T0035581

LEARN HOW TO
RIDE A HORSE

LEARN HOW TO
RIDE A HORSE

A step-by-step riding course from getting started to achieving excellence, illustrated in more than 550 practical photographs

DEBBY SLY

LORENZ BOOKS

CONTENTS

LEARNING TO RIDE

BEFORE CLIMBING
ABOARD

There are few more enviable sights in the world than a horse and rider enjoying a happy, trusting partnership. To be able to harness the spirit and beauty of an animal as majestic as the horse so that he is happy to work with you, and willing to do all that you ask of him, has to be one of life's greatest pleasures. A horse and rider in harmony appear to move by magic, but although the spectator may appreciate the words of Robert Surtees – "there is no closer secret than that between a rider and his horse" – anyone who has experienced some of the setbacks that can occur while trying to acquire the art of horsemanship may wonder whether these words were spoken with admiration, envy or in sheer frustration!

For some, horse riding is an occasional pastime, for others it is a lifelong passion – either way it should be a pleasure for both horse and rider. Learning to ride involves two living creatures – the rider is reliant on the horse's generosity and co-operation; the horse, in return, deserves fair and sensitive treatment from the rider.

IF YOU HAVE NEVER SAT ON A HORSE...

If you have never so much as sat on a horse or pony, there will be a great deal to take in to start with. It will help to have an overall idea in your mind of what it is you are trying to achieve.

Once you have mounted, the means of communication with the horse are through the use of the legs, seat, hands and voice. Anything that you ask the horse to do – from walking forward to performing an intricate dressage movement to jumping a huge fence – is achieved by using a combination of leg, seat, hand and, sometimes, the voice. The art of riding lies in learning to feel what the horse is doing underneath you, and understanding how to influence what he does and how well he performs by mastering this subtle combination of leg, seat and hand. These means of communicating with the horse are called aids. Leg, hand and seat aids, as well as your voice, are called natural aids and they can be backed up by the artificial aids, which are the spur and whip. The spur is a short stump of blunt metal that is worn over the rider's boot just above the heel; the whip is either a short stick or a longer schooling whip. Spurs should not be worn until the rider is proficient enough to control their leg position so that they are able to correctly apply the spur only when needed.

Ultimately, riding a horse should have the same smooth feeling of power and control as driving a high-performance sports car or a speed boat. Just as a powerful car responds instantly to a light touch on the accelerator pedal, a horse should move forward the instant he feels a light squeeze from the rider's leg. The feeling of lightness and control that power steering in a car gives you is the same feeling that a well-schooled horse should give you through the reins. Just an inclination of your hand to guide the horse in one direction or another, or a slight squeeze and hold of the rein to help gather up all his energy and power, is all

■ LEFT
When performing the half-pass you may have to do something different with each hand and leg, which is why attaining an independent seat should be the aim of all riders.

that should be needed. It takes a long period of careful training for a horse to become as responsive as this, and it takes time and practice for a rider to get to the stage of being able to provide that training.

In the beginning, as a general rule of thumb, the novice rider should appreciate that it is the legs that are used first and foremost to instruct the horse to do something. The legs create the power, while the hands gently guide the horse in the right direction.

As a beginner, you will usually find yourself riding in a circle around an instructor. The hand and leg on the inside of the circle are referred to as the inside hand and leg. The hand and leg on the outside of the circle are known as the outside hand and leg. If your inside hand is your left hand, you are said to be riding on the left rein. If you are told to change the rein, this involves turning the horse

around and circling in the opposite direction, so that the inside hand is now your right hand, which means you are now riding on the right rein.

Your arms and hands are linked via the reins to the bit in the horse's mouth. This line of contact is all part of your communication with the horse, and to make life comfortable for him you must aim to relax your arms, so that as the horse's head and neck move you follow that movement. Ideally this is done while still maintaining a consistent but soft contact with the horse's mouth. The idea is not to let the reins keep going slack and then tight, but to relax your arms enough to follow what the horse's head and neck are doing while keeping a constant feel on the reins. The feel that you have down the reins to the horse's mouth is known as the contact, and the ultimate aim is to ride with a very light

AN INDEPENDENT SEAT

The key to all successful riding is to attain what is commonly known as 'an independent seat'. The means of communication with the horse are through your seat, legs, hands and voice – they are six different things and on some occasions you may have to do something different with each of them at the same time! To do this you must be able to sit securely and centrally in the saddle, while leaving your legs and hands free to communicate with the horse. This means being able to keep your balance without gripping with your legs, or hanging on by the reins, at all the gaits. Only then can your legs, seat and hands be used independently of each other to ask the horse to perform some of the more elaborate and enjoyable movements that he can offer you.

In an ideal world, any would-be horseman would first gain this independent seat by riding a horse or pony that is being lunged. To begin with you might hold on to the front of the saddle or to a neck strap to help you keep your balance, but as your body and muscles gradually become used to the movement of the horse underneath you, it becomes easier to remain relaxed and balanced. Various exercises without reins or stirrups will help reinforce the balance and security of your

LEFT
Learning to ride on the lunge is one of the best ways to acquire the feel and balance that are needed to develop an independent seat. Once this is achieved, you can start to ride properly and really influence the horse.

seat until you have attained true independence of hands, seat and legs at all gaits. Lunging can be a tiring and time-consuming operation, besides which, most potential riders are in a rush to enjoy more of the thrill and excitement of horse riding. But if you really want to master the art of riding, it is time well spent, and this will be repaid when you discover how much more effective and sensitive a rider you are when you do progress to more exciting things. Remember – patience and practice are the keys to becoming a successful rider.

contact. It sometimes helps to imagine that the rein is an extension of your arm and that your hands are attached directly to the bit in the horse's mouth. As the horse's head moves, your arms will have to move with him.

However ambitious or casual you may be, by persevering and mastering the correct techniques of horse riding, your satisfaction and enjoyment of your hobby or sport will be greatly enhanced. You may have no desire to reach the dizzy heights

of the competition world – perhaps a simple ride through the countryside is your idea of paradise – but either way, life will be more enjoyable for both you and your horse if you at least attempt to master the art of horsemanship.

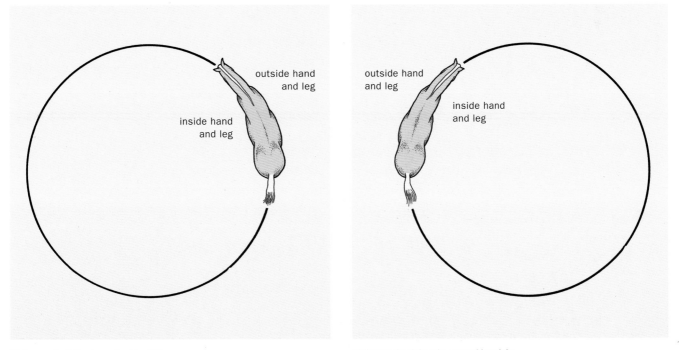

outside hand and leg

inside hand and leg

outside hand and leg

inside hand and leg

Riding on the left rein, or tracking left.

Riding on the right rein, or tracking right.

UNDERSTANDING HORSES AND PONIES

The partnership between a horse and rider should be one of mutual respect. Once you appreciate the size and strength of a horse you will appreciate that the relationship cannot, and should not, be based on force. To safely handle, ride and train a horse or pony you need to understand how the horse sees and understands things. He is a flight animal which means if a situation scares or overwhelms him, his natural reaction is to get away from it as quickly as possible. His senses are far more advanced than ours – he will see, hear and smell things before we do and, depending on his character and training, each horse will react differently to new sights, sounds, and situations.

Much of the secret behind the successful and safe handling of a horse is based on the person being calm and confident, as horses pick up very quickly on the vibes being

Spending time helping to care for and handle horses helps beginners to feel at ease with them.

Enhancing your horse's training by working with him from the ground can be as beneficial as riding him, and sometimes more so.

transmitted by their handlers. If you have little experience of horses, try to spend time getting used to handling and working with them before you start riding them.

The handling and training of the horse must be firm, fair and consistent. From a safety aspect, the horse needs to learn to respect the space around his handler so that he doesn't harm you, accidentally or otherwise, by knocking you over or standing on you. It is the rider's job to teach the

horse what is acceptable and what isn't, and this must be done fairly, consistently and progressively. Your voice and body language are the most valuable tools you have when it comes to influencing and communicating with the horse. Good horsemanship is about understanding how the horse sees and thinks and then using that knowledge to train him in a way that he understands. Natural horsemanship has gained a huge following in recent years but sadly it has created an almost 'them and us' culture in the horse world between 'natural' and 'traditional' horsemanship. However this should not be the case. The word that is important is 'horsemanship' – and, unfortunately, there will always be examples of bad horsemanship in both natural and conventional training. Whatever approach you take, make it your aim to practise good horsemanship. Natural horsemanship is based on understanding the psychology of the horse, and on a system of approach and retreat (moving forwards then moving away), pressure and release (applying pressure to get a response and then removing the pressure to reward the response), rewards and consequences

(rewarding acceptable behaviour, and demonstrating disapproval of unacceptable behaviour), desensitisation (teaching the horse to tolerate and accept situations he may be scared of), and foundation training (teaching a good understanding of the basics before progressing to more challenging work).

These are the words associated with Natural Horsemanship, yet good trainers and riders have always used these principles in their traditional training. Training the horse can be done from the ground and when ridden. Both are valuable forms of training and work well together through all stages of a horse's training. Always bear in mind that if a horse is struggling to do what is asked of him, there is usually a reason, either physical or mental. It is our responsibility to discover the reason, and to then help the horse to progress.

NEAR SIDE, OFF SIDE

Some of the first things to learn in order to avoid confusion all around are the terms used to describe each side of the horse. If you stand facing the same direction as the horse, his left-hand side is known as the near side, and his right-hand side is known as the off side. The horse is led from the near side; you mount and dismount from the near side. The same terms are used to describe each of the horse's limbs – if a horse is said to be lame on his off fore, this refers to the front leg on the right-hand side.

off side   near side

WHERE TO LEARN

Some children are lucky enough to be put on a pony before they can even walk – long before they are in a position to control their ponies off the leading rein, they will have developed a natural seat. This is because someone else has been in charge of the pony – all the rider has had to worry about is staying on board. It is the same principle as being lunged.

For those who haven't had that lucky start, if time and money allow, the best investment is in a course of lunge lessons at an equestrian centre with a good reputation. The advantages of this are that you will be receiving individual attention and, most importantly, you will start to acquire a deep, balanced but relaxed seat in the saddle. Lunging will also give you the opportunity to concentrate on trying to feel how the horse is actually moving underneath you.

There is the danger of the first riding lesson being a miserable experience. Avoid any establishment where novices are put on badly schooled, bored mounts and stuck in a class with any number of other potential riders, and where inexperienced or simply incompetent instructors swagger around shouting instructions or criticism. The poor riders are expected to master

All too often a lack of communication and understanding between horse and rider leads to a lack of co-operation.

the correct riding position, keep their balance in the saddle, and manoeuvre unresponsive creatures around the arena. These new riders will either give up or become insensitive riders, uneducated in the value of true horsemanship.

Lunge lessons will help the rider to develop a good seat, from which he or she will be able to communicate effectively with the horse. For any rider unable to enjoy such an opportunity, the next best thing is to opt for private lessons, rather than group lessons. Once you have mastered the basics, riding in a group can be a positive and enjoyable experience, but if you are just learning to ride, you will benefit most from private lessons right at the beginning. This may either be at a commercial riding school or equestrian centre, or with an individual who may give lessons using their own horses and facilities.

Always ensure that the instructor of your choice has a good reputation both for teaching ability and for being safe and responsible. In most countries there is some form of recognized teaching body and a structured system of examinations for instructors; if you have nobody to advise you, always opt for a registered and approved instructor. But if someone is highly recommended to you by more experienced riders, do not be afraid to try them even if teaching is not their profession – some people are naturally gifted teachers.

With a willing helper to lead the way, the world is yours to explore. It is a great advantage to learn to ride at such an early age. There are classes for young riders on lead reins at most equestrian centres.

Group riding lessons are beneficial and fun once the potential rider has had a chance to master some of the basics.

CLOTHING AND EQUIPMENT

HARD HAT

One vital item that the rider must have is a hard riding hat, also known as a crash hat or skull cap, which conforms to a recognized safety standard. Any romantic notions about feeling the wind blowing through your hair, or galloping across the prairie in your designer stetson should be dismissed – it is only fair to yourself, and to those who will have to pick up the pieces if you have an accident, that you wear the correct headgear. The design and effectiveness of riding hats has improved dramatically. A riding hat must always be worn with a safety harness to hold it in place; a traditional hard hat with an elastic chin strap is next to useless.

Hard hats come in various designs – looking like the traditional velvet hat with a built-in peak, or like a crash hat or skull cap as worn by racing jockeys and cross-country riders. The latter are more bulbous looking than the traditional type. Some of the newest styles, popularized in America, are very lightweight, vented helmets which protect the head whilst allowing the rider to stay surprisingly cool.

Riding helmets are being improved continually. The highest current safety standards are SNELL E2001, ASTM F1163, AS/NZS 3838 (2006 onwards), VG01.040 (2014) and PAS 015 (1998/2011). A new standard EN14572 is under development, which will include a new crush test.

The majority of approved riding or training centres insist that their clients wear protective headgear and, similarly, whenever a rider competes he or she will generally be required to wear a proper hat. A riding hat should always be replaced once it has suffered a hard blow, either through the rider falling, or through being dropped accidentally.

RIDING BOOTS

The second most important item of clothing, from a safety point of view, is footwear. Long or short boots of some kind should be worn; it is important that they are not so wide that there is any risk of them being caught in the stirrup in the event of a fall, and they should only have a small heel – again so that there is no risk of the rider's foot becoming trapped.

The jockey-style crash hat or skull cap can be worn on its own, or you can fit a 'silk' to it – dark blue or black for dressage and show jumping, and a colour to match your outfit for cross-country riding. Whatever style of hat you choose, it MUST fit your head correctly to be of any use.

Jodhpurs are usually made of a stretchy material and are designed to be worn with short boots.

Breeches are designed to be worn with long riding boots.

This vented riding hat, with a soft peak, is suitable for everyday riding, as well as for show jumping and dressage.

Lightweight, ventilated helmets are a popular choice, particularly for endurance riding.

Short leather jodhpur boots can be worn with jodhpurs or with a pair of 'half-chaps' to protect the rider's lower leg.

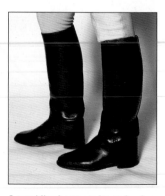

Long riding boots can be made of either rubber or leather.

It is advisable to carry a stick of some sort even if you think you are unlikely to need it. It is too late if you go out without one and your horse decides on that particular day to ignore your leg aids. From top to bottom: hunting whip, two types of riding sticks, and a schooling whip.

You can buy casual riding footwear for leisure riding, but for competition riding you would generally wear long leather or rubber riding boots.

GLOVES
Most riders like to wear gloves. These should have non-slip palms.

TROUSERS
For the sake of comfort, wear trousers designed specifically for riding. Any garment with a thick seam will chafe against your skin, and anything too thin or flimsy will simply wear through. Jodhpurs or breeches come in a huge variety of styles and colours, and can be purchased as either competition or casual garments.

CHAPS
If short boots are to be worn, it is also advisable to wear what are known as chaps or half-chaps, which are shaped leggings made from leather, suede or waterproof material. Half-chaps are worn below the

■ RIGHT
Whatever type of gloves you choose, make sure that they have non-slip palms; otherwise the reins will slip through your fingers.

If spurs are worn, they should be as short as possible and should have a rounded, blunt or rollerball end. They should not be worn until the rider has good control of their lower leg position, otherwise they will not be able to differentiate between using the spur and not using it.

Protective clothing is important for both horse and rider. This rider is wearing a jockey-style crash helmet with safety harness, a body protector and long leather riding boots. Her horse is wearing protective leg boots to reduce the risk of injury through knocking into himself, or being scratched or cut by anything whilst being ridden.

A neck strap can prove invaluable as an aid to staying in the saddle if the horse plays up or jumps awkwardly. Hold on to the strap with one hand to help keep your weight deep in the saddle, making it harder for you to be thrown off. It can also be used as an aid to help slow the horse down.

knee and protect the lower leg. They are usually fastened by either Velcro or a zip, and prevent the stirrup leather rubbing against the rider's calf. Full chaps are just like the ones cowboys wear; they cover the whole leg and are fastened with a belt around the waist. As well as offering some protection to the leg, they have the advantage of keeping the rider warm.

BODY PROTECTOR
These are padded, vest-like garments and are mandatory in most countries for sports such as horse racing and the cross-country phase of horse trials. The lastest lightweight breatheable materials ensure that they are nothing like as cumbersome and hot as they used to be. A body protector, along with a good riding helmet, can save your life in the event of a fall and it is no bad thing to wear one for all your riding activities. The newest standards are EN13158, ASTM F1937 and ASTM F2681. There is also a BETA standard which grades body protectors from a protection level of one to three.

Inflatable air jackets are becoming popular; an attachment from the body protector to the saddle triggers a gas cylinder to inflate the body protector as the rider falls from the saddle. But these must be worn over a standard body protector just in case the trigger mechanism fails.

NECK STRAP
A final, small piece of equipment that also adds to the rider's safety is a neck strap, which is worn by the horse. This is a leather strap (an old stirrup leather makes an ideal neck strap) worn loosely around the horse's neck. It sits just above the withers and is well positioned for you to grab hold of if you lose your balance, and can make the difference between staying on and falling off. They will also reduce the risk of you jabbing the horse in the mouth if you lose your balance jumping, and can be used when you are riding as a 'braking' aid by giving a little tug on the neck strap rather than using a stronger rein aid.

SITTING COMFORTABLY

Before you even get as far as sitting on a horse there is quite
a lot of groundwork to master, such as tacking up and
mounting. Riding schools vary in their approach to tacking
up for beginners. Some have the horse ready and waiting
for his rider; others feel that tacking up is all part of the
learning process and that it will give you a few minutes of
unpressured time in which to start to get to know your
horse. If a friend is teaching you, it is all part of the fun
to help get the horse ready.

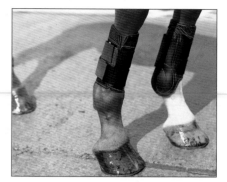

TACKING UP

The order in which the horse is tacked up varies, but any form of boots should be put on first, once the horse's legs have been checked for signs of heat or swelling. This should have been done while the horse was being groomed, but it is good practice to double check when putting on the boots – there is no point tacking up and then finding that the horse is lame!

Whether the saddle or bridle is put on next is a matter for discussion. Some riders like to put the bridle on first, so that they have better control of the horse should he pull back and break free from his headcollar (halter). Others like to put the saddle on first so that, having removed the horse's rug (blanket), the saddle goes straight on to a warm back and the horse's muscles will remain warm underneath the saddle. On a cold day, a rug should be kept over the horse's back and quarters while he is being tacked up.

Protective boots reduce the risk of injury. Hold the boot securely in place and fasten the first strap. Then fasten the second strap firmly enough to prevent the boot from slipping. Tighten the first strap if it seems looser than the second strap. These boots protect the tendon area of the legs as well as the inside of the fetlocks. Many horses are prone to knocking one leg against the inside of the opposite leg – this is called brushing – and boots prevent the horse from injuring himself as a result.

PUTTING ON THE BRIDLE

1 While being tacked up or groomed, the horse is usually secured by a headcollar (halter). Before removing the headcollar, put the reins over the horse's head so that you have a means of holding him.

2 Remove the headcollar by lifting the headpiece (crownpiece) forward and then gently lifting it over the horse's ears.

3 With one hand holding the horse's nose to keep his head steady, bring the bridle up in front of his face.

4 Use your right hand to hold the bridle, lay the bit over the palm of your left hand and gently lift it up into the horse's mouth. Use your thumb to press his gum in the gap where his teeth end which will encourage him to open his mouth.

5 Once the bit is in place, keep some tension on each side of the bridle to hold it there while you bring the headpiece of the bridle up and over the horse's ears. Do not allow the bit to bang against his teeth, as this will make him wary next time.

6 With the headpiece in place, separate the hair of the forelock from the rest of the mane (to let the bridle sit comfortably, cut a small section out of the mane where the headpiece sits). Bring the forelock forward and lift it clear of the browband.

7 Keep your hand looped through the rein so that you have a contact with the horse, and therefore control over him, and then do up the throatlash.

8 It should not be fastened too tightly – make sure you can still get four fingers of your hand between the horse's cheek and the throatlash.

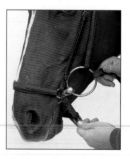

9 Fasten the noseband – in this case a drop noseband that fastens below the bit rings. A cavesson noseband sits higher up the horse's nose and fastens above the bit rings.

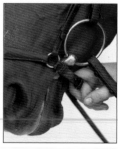

10 You should be able to place at least one finger between the horse's chin and the noseband.

SADDLING UP

1 Place a soft, clean numnah on the horse's back. This acts as a cushion between the horse and the saddle and can reduce the risk of rubbing. It is also a warmer layer to have against the horse's skin than the leather of the saddle.

2 Keeping the saddle well clear of the horse's back, lift it so that it is poised in the right position to be lowered on to the back. Lower the saddle into place, making sure that the saddle flap on the off side is lying flat.

3 Use your left hand to lift the numnah so that it is not pulled tight over the horse's withers. It should be tucked up to lie snugly under the pommel of the saddle, clear of the withers. Now slide the saddle and numnah back so that the panels are clear of the horse's shoulder blade.

4 Most numnahs have two straps that hold them in position under the saddle. The first one is usually attached to the girth straps (billets), so pull it over the knee roll of the saddle and put it on the billet before you fasten the girth.

5 Position the strap above the buckle guard; otherwise you will not be able to pull this down into the correct position. Pull the girth strap out from the buckle guard, thread through the numnah strap, then put the strap back through the buckle guard.

6 Buckle the girth to the saddle on the off side. Return to the near side, and reach under the horse's belly to catch the girth. Thread the girth buckles through the second securing strap of the numnah and fasten them, one at a time, to each girth strap.

7 Gently tighten the girth, one buckle at a time, until you can just squeeze the flat of your hand between the horse's belly and the girth. Fasten the girth equally on each side.

8 Pull the buckle guard down so that it covers the buckles – otherwise they will gradually wear a hole through the saddle flap.

9 Slide your hand under the girth just clear of the saddle flap and run it down under the horse's belly, taking particular care to smooth any wrinkles in the horse's elbow area. Lift each front leg and draw it forwards to ensure there are no wrinkles of skin trapped under the girth.

10 A correctly fitted jumping saddle, with the girth tightened and the stirrups run up so that they don't swing and bang against the horse's sides. A jumping saddle has forward-cut flaps and knee rolls to allow the rider to keep his or her leg on the saddle even when riding with shorter stirrups.

PUTTING ON A DRESSAGE SADDLE

1 A dressage saddle has long girth straps that fasten below the saddle flap. The girth must still be tightened gradually, one buckle at a time, and the skin and hair smoothed down underneath it.

2 Dressage saddles allow your legs to hang much longer and closer to the horse's sides. This gives the best possible position for you to communicate with the horse through your legs and seat.

LEADING A TACKED-UP HORSE

When leading a tacked-up horse, stand on his near side and bring the reins over his head. The stirrups should be run up so that they do not swing or bang against the horse's sides. Carry the excess loop of rein and your riding stick, if you are carrying one, in your left hand. Have the stick pointing backward so you can give the horse a tap behind the girth if he refuses to walk on. You should always wear a helmet whenever you lead a horse.

MOUNTING

So now it is time to step aboard. It is essential to learn how to mount correctly from the ground but, as a general rule, it is far less stressful on the horse's back to use a mounting block or be given a leg-up. Either of these methods is also a lot safer than mounting from the ground. Many accidents occur when riders are trying to get on their horses. If you do mount from the ground, ideally an assistant should stand on the far side of the horse and, by putting his or her hand in the stirrup iron, should use some of his or her own weight to counteract your weight swinging up from the other side. This helps to reduce the amount of twisting and pulling on the horse's spine.

1 Whichever way you are going to mount, you will need to put the reins back over the horse's head and let down the stirrups. As you pull the stirrup irons down, keep them away from the horse's sides so that they don't bump him. When they are fully down, place them gently back against his sides. Stand on the near side of the horse, facing his tail and put both reins in your left hand. It also helps to loop a finger through the neck strap and hold on to a little piece of the mane.

2 Use your right hand to take hold of the stirrup. Turn it clockwise to face you, so that once you are mounted the stirrup leather will lie correctly against the saddle flap. Place your left foot in the stirrup.

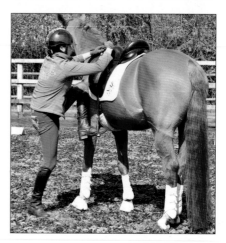

3 Place your right hand on the pommel of the saddle or, if you can reach, grasp the far side of the seat of the saddle.

4 Push off the ground with your right leg, trying to create as much spring as possible, and reach over with your right hand to hold the back of the saddle to help balance yourself.

5 Lift your right leg until it is well clear of the saddle, then move your right hand forwards to the front of the saddle and start to bring your right leg down on the far side of the horse.

6 Lower your seat gently down into the saddle. Put your right foot in the stirrup and pick up a rein in each hand.

GETTING A LEG-UP

1 If someone is going to give you a leg-up on to your horse, you should stand on the near side facing the saddle. Take both reins and your stick in your left hand – making sure you carry the stick down over the off-side shoulder of the horse; otherwise you will hit your helper in the face with it as you mount up! Rest your left hand on the horse's neck or on the pommel of the saddle, and reach up with your right hand so that it is resting near the back of the saddle.

2 Bend your left leg from the knee and lift your foot up so that your help can take hold of your lower leg with both hands.

3 When your helper gives the command, spring up off your right leg. They will support and lift your left leg at the same time. Take your weight on your hands to balance your upper body and to control the moment when you want to swing your right leg over the horse's back.

4 When you have gained enough height to clear the horse's back, start to swing your right leg over.

USING A MOUNTING BLOCK

◾ LEFT
It is far less stressful for both horse and rider if you are able to get aboard by using a mounting block. The horse is led alongside the mounting block so that his near side is parallel to the block. Use the stirrup to mount in the normal way. Now that you are that much higher off the ground, there is less strain on the horse's back when you step up into the stirrup.

5 As you swing your leg over the back of the horse, move your right hand from the back of the saddle to the front to support your weight, as you lower yourself down on to the saddle.

ADJUSTING TACK

Having learned how to tack up and mount your horse, there are one or two other small adjustments you will need to make once you are on board. The first thing you must do is tighten the girth. Although this is tightened from the ground before you mount, your weight pushing the saddle down on to the horse's back will cause the girth to need retightening. Also, many horses push their stomachs out against the pressure of the girth, and only relax again once their riders are in the saddle.

It is only once you are sitting on your horse that you can feel if your stirrups are set at a comfortable length for you; they may need adjusting. When you change from riding on the flat to jumping you will also want to shorten your stirrups while still sitting on the horse.

TIGHTENING THE GIRTH

1 To retighten the girth, put both reins and your stick in your right hand and bring your left leg clear of the saddle flap.

2 Reach down and lift up the saddle flap so that you have access to the girth straps (billets).

3 Hold the saddle flap out of the way with your right hand; with your left hand, pull the buckle guard up away from the girth straps and buckles.

4 Take hold of the first girth strap and pull it up gently. Use your index finger to press the spike of the buckle through the hole.

5 Do the same to the second girth strap – make sure each is tightened by the same number of holes.

6 Pull the buckle guard back down so that it sits snugly over the girth buckles. Put the saddle flap back down and return your leg to the correct position.

HOLDING THE REINS

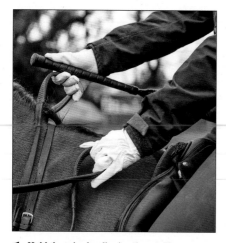  

1 Hold the reins by allowing them to lie across the palm of your hand. The end that comes from the horse's mouth passes between your third and fourth finger.

2 It rests over the top of your first finger and is held in place by closing your thumb and fingers. You can lengthen the reins by relaxing the tension in your hand and letting them slip through your fingers.

3 This picture shows you how to hold a stick as well as your reins. When your thumb and fingers close back around the rein and stick, they are held safely in place.

ADJUSTING THE STIRRUP LEATHERS

1 Once you are in the saddle you may need to adjust your stirrup leathers in order to sit comfortably and correctly. Put the reins and stick in your right hand, and use your left hand to lift the leather flap that covers the stirrup-leather buckle.

2 Pull the free end of the stirrup leather out of its keeper if necessary, and then pull it upward so that the buckle is released.

3 To shorten your stirrup, pull the stirrup leather upward, as shown. To lengthen your stirrup, put your weight down into the stirrup iron and with your left hand allow the stirrup leather to slide back down through the stirrup bar.

4 When the stirrup is at the required length, push the buckle back through the appropriate hole.

5 Make sure the stirrup-leather buckle slides back into position against the stirrup bar.

6 Push the free end of the stirrup leather back through the keeper.

7 Ensure that the leather is lying flat before repeating the procedure for the right stirrup.

POSITIONING THE STIRRUP LEATHER

Each stirrup leather should be turned outward, rather than inward, in order to position the stirrup iron so that your foot can go into it. This allows the stirrup leather to curve smoothly across the inside of your leg. So to put your right foot (off-side foot) in the stirrup iron, give the leather a quarter turn in a clockwise direction. For the near-side foot (left foot), turn the stirrup leather in an anti-clockwise direction.

4 You should always hold both your hands at the same height, usually just above the withers and a few inches apart. The basic rule for hand position is that there should be a straight line running from your elbow, down your arm, through the wrist and hand, down the rein to the horse's mouth. It is this rule that dictates the exact position of your hands, which will therefore alter depending on what the horse is doing with his head carriage. This hand and arm position allows you to maintain a soft, elastic but consistent contact with the horse's mouth. (See The Hands, opposite, which illustrates three different but correct positions.)

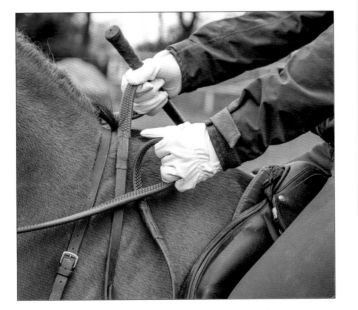

DISMOUNTING

As with mounting, dismounting from the horse should be done correctly. Do not be tempted to follow the example of countless cowboys in Wild West movies by flinging your leg over the front of the saddle. If the horse throws his head up you will, at best, be knocked off backward or, at worst, startle the horse so that he either jumps or bolts, leading to even more painful consequences. Always remove both feet from the stirrups, lean forward and swing your right leg up and over behind the saddle. As obvious as it may sound, always check that the ground where you are about to land is safe and free of obstacles before you dismount. Also look around to check there is nothing that might startle your horse as you dismount.

GETTING OFF

1 Take both feet out of the stirrups, put the reins (and stick) in your left hand, and place both hands on the pommel of the saddle. Bend your upper body forward and start to swing your right leg up and over the back of the horse.

2 Use your arms to support and balance the weight of your upper body as you continue to swing your right leg over the horse's back. Swing your left leg back and out slightly so that it meets your right leg as it comes down over the near side of the horse.

3 Use your hands and arms to push your upper body away from the horse so that you do not land right underneath him.

4 As you land, bend both your knees to help absorb the impact. Sometimes it's a long way down!

THE IDEAL POSITION

Once on the horse, you should try to adopt a proud and elegant posture. The ideal, classical position is like that of a person standing with their knees slightly bent, not sitting in an armchair. Your ear, shoulder, hip and heel should all be in line, with equal weight placed on each seat bone so that you are not tipped too far forward or sitting back on your buttocks. Always remember how heavy your head is in relation to the rest of your body – if you look down, or tilt your head to the side, or push it too far forward, it will affect your, and therefore the horse's, balance. Your legs should hang long and loose down the horse's sides. When your foot is balanced in the stirrup, think of allowing your weight to sink down into your heel.

Although it is often frowned upon today by many who consider it unsafe, anyone who was fortunate enough to learn to ride bareback tends to adopt a correct position automatically. Often, it is the addition of the saddle and the stirrups which compromises what was otherwise a near-perfect position.

By practicing the ideal position on the ground, you can start to get a good feel of what you are aiming for, before the added complication of the movement of the horse underneath you enters the equation. Similarly, while sitting on the stationary horse, you can be shown how to follow the movement of his head and neck, so that you do not restrict the horse or harm him by pulling on the reins in an attempt to keep your balance.

Your foot should be balanced centrally in the stirrup, with the stirrup tread positioned under the ball of your foot and your weight lowered gently down into your heel.

If you sit a child on a pony bareback, his or her leg position will automatically be long and low as required for the classical position.

As soon as a saddle is introduced, note how the child adopts an armchair seat. The best way to acquire a natural, classical seat is to learn to ride either bareback or without stirrups.

1 You can practise the classical riding position on the ground. First stand straight, with your legs about 2 feet (0.5 m) apart, and your arms bent at the elbow as if you were holding the horse's reins.

2 Keeping your whole body straight and upright, simply bend your knees slightly – now you are in the classical dressage position. For jumping you simply bend your knees more. Your position on a horse should be as if you were standing with your knees bent, rather than as if you were sitting in a chair.

▮ LEFT

Your position in the saddle should be exactly the same as the position you have practised on the ground. See how this rider appears to be standing with her knees bent rather than sitting on the saddle. Note how there is a straight line through the rider's ear, shoulder, hip and heel. Similarly there is another straight line running from the elbow, down through the wrist and hand to the rein and eventually to the bit.

COMMON FAULTS

How not to sit! You should not allow your weight to fall on to the back of your buttocks as if you were sitting on a chair. Note how, when this happens, the rider's lower leg swings forward and becomes ineffective as a result.

You should not sit with your weight pitched forward. It prevents you from sitting properly and using your legs correctly – and it is painful! Note how this position causes the lower leg to slide back.

PRACTISING A SOFT CONTACT

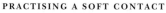

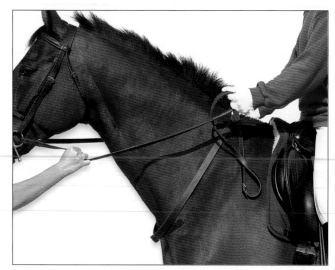

1 One of the secrets of sympathetic and effective riding is to learn how to maintain a soft but constant contact with the horse's mouth, while allowing him to move his head and neck freely. Take up a rein in each hand, and ask a friend to hold the rein further down toward the horse's mouth.

2 Ask your friend to mimic the movement of the horse's head and neck by drawing the rein forward and then releasing it. Concentrate on maintaining the straight line from your elbow, through your wrist and hand down the rein. Keep your elbows and wrists soft and relaxed, and allow your whole arm, from the shoulder down, to be moved by the pull on the reins.

THE HANDS

Never forget that your hands are attached directly, via the reins, to a large piece of metal in the horse's mouth. Like your own, the horse's mouth is soft and sensitive, and you must never be harsh or abusive with your hands. One of the most important ideas to grasp is that your hands belong to the horse's mouth. Although a light, consistent contact must be maintained so that you have a line of communication with the horse, that contact should be elastic. Your hands must follow the movement of the horse's head and neck. It should feel as if you are shaking hands politely with someone; there is equal pressure and movement from each party. It is not polite to clasp someone's hand roughly and shake it as violently as a terrier might shake a rat! Nor is it kind to grasp the reins and swing and tug on them.

When a horse is working correctly, the energy created by his hindlegs is contained and controlled by your hands on the reins – this is what the connection is. The connection may sometimes be very strong as the horse will create a lot of power, but it must always be elastic so that the horse feels he has the freedom to

COMMON FAULTS

A common fault is to have stiff, straight arms and to turn the wrists and hands outward. You can see from this position how harsh this looks, and how impossible it would be to keep a sympathetic contact with the horse.

A similar error is to carry your hands so that the thumbs are pointing downward – again, this prevents you from maintaining a soft, consistent contact with the horse's mouth.

move forwards. This is achieved by allowing your arms to be relaxed enough to allow the horse to draw the contact forwards while still controlling the energy you have asked him to create.

The exact position of the hands, and how close they are held to the withers, depends upon the horse's head carriage. There should always be a straight line from the elbow, through the wrist, down the rein to the bit; so, if the horse is working with his head quite low, the

hands must be carried a little lower and to either side of the withers in order to keep this straight line. When the horse is working in a rounder frame, the hands can be carried a little higher, and when you find yourself riding a highly schooled horse who carries his head and neck higher still, your hands should be carried a few inches above the withers. The rule of thumb is to be aware of keeping the straight line from the elbow, through the rein to the horse's mouth.

You must adjust your arm position, following the horse's head and neck, so that you maintain an imaginary straight line from your elbow, through your wrist and hand, down the rein to the bit.

When you encourage the horse to stretch and lower his neck, you must still keep the straight line. This rider has allowed her arms and elbows to be drawn forward and down so that the line is maintained.

Here, the horse is working with more pronounced flexion and bend through his neck. In this case you should raise your lower arms and hands slightly to maintain the line.

THE LEGS

The most important way that you can communicate with the horse is through the legs and seat. Your legs should hang long and relaxed around the horse's sides, with no tightness in the knee joints in particular. It is the insides of the calves that squeeze against the horse to ask him to move either forward or across to one side or the other. If you run your hand down the inside of your leg just below the knee, you should feel the slight outward bulge of your calf muscle; it is this part of the leg that is used to communicate with the horse.

Check that your stirrup length is correct by allowing each leg to hang long and loose, and free of the stirrup. You should then only need to turn your toe up slightly to find the stirrup. This is the position that you should be aiming for,

Ask a friend to adjust the stirrup leather so that you only need to turn up your toe to find the stirrup iron. It may take some time for you to be able to ride comfortably with such a long stirrup length as your muscles will need to supple up and stretch, but this is what you are aiming for.

although at first it is likely to produce too much pull down the back of the thigh and calf muscles. Until your muscles have toned, stretched and strengthened sufficiently, it is sensible to ride with the leg in as long a position as is still comfortable. With time, and particularly as you begin to find your balance on the horse and the beginnings of an independent seat, you will gradually find it easier to ride with the leg in a longer position.

Keep your knee joint relaxed and let it fall away from the saddle slightly, which will allow the leg to hang correctly around the horse's side. Contrary to popular belief, you should not grip with the knees, as doing so will effectively push your seat up and out of the saddle. Equally, if you hold your knees tightly against the saddle, you cannot squeeze the horse's sides with your legs. The knee and the toe have to be turned slightly outward to allow the inside of the calf to press against the horse's sides, which you will need to do to apply a leg aid correctly.

A common fault is for the lower leg to be drawn back and upward in order to press against the horse's side, but this is an

To find the correct stirrup length that will allow you to adopt the classical position for flatwork, you should sit deep in the saddle and just allow your legs to hang long and loose without putting them in the stirrups.

This is the classical position viewed from the front. You can see how the rider's legs would completely encompass the body of the horse; it is this position that allows the leg to support the horse at all times, and from which you can communicate with the horse through your leg aids.

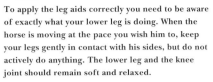

LEFT
To apply the leg aids correctly you need to be aware of exactly what your lower leg is doing. When the horse is moving at the pace you wish him to, keep your legs gently in contact with his sides, but do not actively do anything. The lower leg and the knee joint should remain soft and relaxed.

ineffective means of communication. The lower leg must lie close to the girth; it will come into contact with the part of the horse's belly which is fractionally behind the girth. For some movements, such as turning, or when the rider wants to control the horse's hindquarters, the lower leg is used a few inches further back behind the girth. But the leg is always used in the same way – with the weight down in the heel, the knee and toe turned out slightly and with a squeeze or nudge inward, not backward. If you conjure up in your mind a picture of an old-fashioned, bow-legged horseman, you will have a good idea of how the rider's legs are used against the horse's sides, and why some riders end up looking bow-legged!

COMMON FAULTS

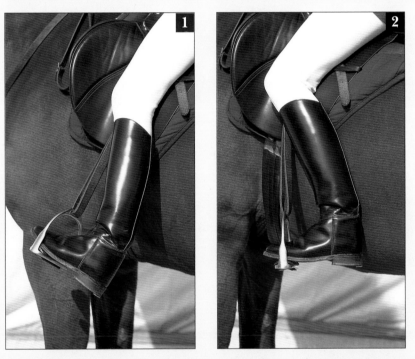

When you wish to apply a leg aid, simply squeeze your lower leg inward. Allow your knee to come slightly away from the saddle so that your lower leg may close in against the horse's side. Your weight remains gently pushed down into your heel. Again you can get a feel for this by asking a friend to push your leg inward against the horse's sides. Having your leg held in the right position will give you a feel for what you are trying to achieve. Until your muscles are used to this movement it will seem difficult, and you will not be able to apply a very strong leg aid. Your thigh and calf muscles will need to stretch and strengthen before your leg aids can be truly effective.

Picture one shows a bad leg position – see how the lower leg is pushed forward and away from the horse's sides. This is usually a result of the rider adopting an armchair seat in the saddle. It leads to the leg aids being incorrectly applied.

In picture two, instead of squeezing inward this rider has drawn her lower leg back and, as a result, her weight has come out of her heel and her heel is higher than her toe. At this point it is very easy for the stirrup iron to slip off your foot. This type of leg aid is ineffective – the lower leg is simply being brushed backward across the horse's side and is not being applied to the more sensitive area just behind the girth. A horse that is ridden like this will never be able to differentiate between an aid to move forward and an aid to move his quarters, when the rider's lower leg is applied further back behind the girth.

LUNGING EXERCISES

The handler keeps a contact with the horse via the lunge line. The lunge whip can be used behind the horse's hindquarters to encourage him to move forward, or it can be flicked toward his shoulder to keep him out on the circle. Both rider and handler should wear a riding hat; the handler should also wear gloves.

One of the best ways to encourage an independent seat is to be lunged. When the horse is lunged, the handler on the ground can control the horse's speed and direction, leaving you free to concentrate fully on your position. Lunge lessons are given at most riding establishments. It is important that the horse you ride is calm and steady on the lunge, and that the person who is lunging you is capable and confident in what they are doing. A lunging cavesson should be used over the horse's usual bridle. This is like a padded halter with a reinforced piece on the noseband that has rings attached to it. These take the lunge line. The handler should maintain a position that allows the lunge line, the lunging whip and the horse to form a triangle.

The voice rather than the lunge whip should be used to ask the horse to move forward. The lunge whip should only be used to back up the voice if the horse does not respond, and then should be moved quietly so that the horse does not suddenly shoot forward. He should be allowed to settle into a steady rhythm; this will make it easier for you to relax and find your balance. Both horse and rider should be allowed periods of rest during these exercises.

Lunging should only ever take place on a secure surface. If you only have a field and it is hard and rutted, or deep and wet, the horse is likely to injure or strain his tendons if he is made to work on it. Lunge lessons should not last for more than 20–30 minutes, and work should be carried out in both directions. Working on a circle is tiring and stressful to the horse's limbs, and once you are tired or sore you will not be able to do anything more to improve your position. If anything, it will get worse as you tense up with effort. If you are struggling, it is much better to stop than to keep going until you reach the point of exhaustion or frustration.

RIDING WITHOUT STIRRUPS

Although work without stirrups is usually carried out on the lunge, or in an arena or *manège*, if you have the opportunity to hack out regularly, it is worth making yourself ride for a few minutes each time without stirrups. Normally, the stirrups would be crossed over in front of the saddle so that they don't bang against the horse's sides, but this is not advisable out on a hack in case you need the stirrups back in a hurry. You should only ride without stirrups on a hack at walk. At this gait they should not swing so much that they knock the horse's sides or elbows. Equally, you can quickly slip them back on if necessary. After only a few minutes of riding without stirrups, when you put your feet back in them they often feel too short – that is the time to let the stirrup leathers down a hole so that gradually you can ride at a longer length.

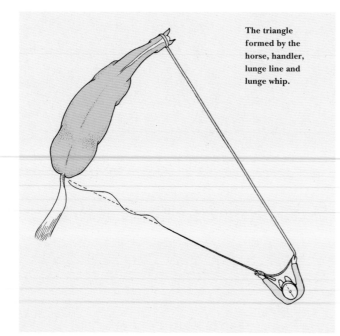

The triangle formed by the horse, handler, lunge line and lunge whip.

To help stretch the thigh muscles, practise this simple exercise. Bring your feet up under your seat and hold them in position with a hand around each ankle. This has the added advantage of helping you to keep your shoulders up and straight, and it automatically puts your seat in the correct position in the saddle. When you take your stirrups back after these exercises, you may feel that you want to lengthen the stirrup leathers. This is a good sign and is the start of the path toward attaining the classical position.

STRENGTHENING EXERCISE

1 Practise riding without stirrups and, to help build up your confidence and balance, spread your arms out to either side.

2 To help strengthen and supple your upper body, twist first around to the left . . .

3 . . . and then back to the right.

HOLDING THE LUNGE LINE

1 It is important that whoever is going to lunge you knows how to do this safely and correctly. One of the biggest risks to the handler is getting his or her hands trapped in the lunge line should the horse panic and try to run away. The safest way to hold the lunge line is not to loop it around your hand but to do the following: Lay the end of the lunge line across the palm of your hand. Do not put your hand through the loop that most lunge lines have on the end.

2 Lay the lunge line, in equal loops, backward and forward across the palm of your hand. Continue to loop the line across your palm until it is the desired length, i.e. you are the distance you want to be away from the horse.

3 Now you can close your hand around the loops and keep a contact with the horse as he moves. If you want to let more lunge line out so that the horse can work on a larger circle, just open your hand and allow one loop to fall away. If the horse did panic and pull away you could close your hand tight around the line and try to stop him. But if he has built up too much speed and is determined to get away, the lunge line will be pulled out of your hand, and you will be free of it. If it is looped around your hand and the horse bolts, the loops will tighten like a noose around your hand. You will either be dragged or have your fingers torn off. Either way the horse will escape if he is determined, so it is better to let him go if you have to and at least remain in one piece and in a position to retrieve him.

'AROUND THE WORLD' EXERCISE

◾ LEFT
The horse or pony you learn to ride on should be a sensible and calm one. This young rider is making the most of her pony's kind nature to have some fun, while also increasing her confidence on horseback. Exercises such as this one – called 'Around the World' – should only ever be carried out on a quiet pony and with someone on the ground to hold the pony's head.

Mastering the Gaits

Having climbed aboard, it is now time to experience some forward motion! The first thing you will suddenly be aware of is just how much the horse moves underneath you. The horse has four legs to operate and, at walk, these move one at a time. As each shoulder or hindquarter swings the appropriate leg forward, you will feel it. Each gait (or pace) the horse can offer you – walk, trot, canter and gallop – will give a different sensation of speed and motion, and you must learn to absorb it, and to remain balanced on the horse at each gait while still maintaining the correct, classical position. To the outside eye, horse and rider should appear to be moving as one.

ABSORBING THE MOVEMENT

In an attempt to follow the movement of the horse, many riders end up trying too hard and do too much with their bodies. This, instead of creating a picture of harmony, actually looks completely unco-ordinated; the horse appears to be moving to one beat, and the rider to another. It is also uncomfortable.

The first thing to bear in mind is that your seat belongs to the saddle which, in turn, belongs to the horse's back. The saddle will mimic the movement of the horse's back and you should imagine that your seat is glued to the saddle. Sit deep in the saddle, with your weight distributed equally on each seat bone. When striving for a deep, balanced seat, it sometimes helps to imagine that your legs have been cut off, about halfway down the thigh; therefore it is the top half of the thighs and the seat itself that embrace the saddle. By sitting up straight and keeping the shoulders balanced above the hips, your

weight sinks down into the saddle. This allows the legs to hang long and loose around the horse's sides, with the foot supported softly by the stirrup. The arms follow the movement of the horse's head and neck, and this is achieved by keeping the elbows soft and relaxed with your shoulders remaining still. If your seat is glued to the saddle, and your shoulders, head and neck remain still, the only part of your body that is free to move is the area between your hips and your ribcage. So the hips and stomach are rocked gently forward and back by the movement of the horse. It is by being soft and supple through the hips, the lower back and the stomach that you are able to move as one with the horse. Always remember that it is the horse that moves your body, and so your body must remain relaxed to allow it to be moved by the horse. You should not create any additional movement yourself – this is most likely to happen if your body is tense.

THE WALK

The walk is described as a four-beat gait because the horse moves each leg individually; if you listen to his footfalls you hear four separate hoofbeats. At the trot, the horse moves his legs in diagonal pairs, so this is known as a two-beat gait.

The sequence of footfalls at the walk is as follows: outside hind, outside fore, inside hind, inside fore. The horse should take strides of equal length and he should look energetic and purposeful. If you watch a horse walking you will see that his whole body is in action; the movement flows through the muscles of the hindquarters, up over the back, and through the shoulders and the neck. The horse should look supple, athletic and powerful. Although the walk is the horse's slowest gait, he does use his neck to quite a degree, which means you must be particularly aware of allowing your arms to follow the movement so that you do not restrict the horse.

MOVING WITH THE HORSE

At the walk the rider allows his hips and stomach to be rocked gently forward and back by the push of the horse's hindquarters beneath him. Notice how the rider is maintaining a straight line from the elbow, through the lower arm, and down the rein to the bit. A light but constant contact is kept with the horse's mouth by allowing the arms to follow the natural movement of the horse's head and neck as he walks.

HALT TO WALK AND WALK TO HALT

TRANSITIONS

Changing gaits on a horse, whether it be from halt to walk, or from trot to canter etc, is known as performing a transition. Like shifting gears in a car, whether you are increasing or decreasing pace, it should appear smooth and effortless.

Transitions are achieved by a subtle balance of the use of the hand and leg. Use your lower leg to activate the horse's hindquarters, which is where his power comes from. You can then use your hands to guide that power in whichever direction you wish.

■ REFINING THE USE OF THE LEGS AND HANDS

To walk forward, squeeze your legs against the horse's sides and allow your hands and arms to be drawn forward. If the horse ignores you, give him a sharper nudge with your heels. If this is ignored, give him a tap with the schooling whip or stick behind your lower leg. If you have to do

1 At the halt the rider still keeps a light contact with the horse's mouth and lets the legs hang long and loose by the horse's sides. The lower leg is in contact with the horse but is not actively doing anything. Note how a straight line is maintained from the shoulder to the hip to the heel. The position would be better still if the rider kept her chin up – a common fault of many riders is the tendency to look down!

2 To go forward to the walk, the rider squeezes both legs against the horse's sides and, at the same time, allows the hands and arms to go forward to follow the forward movement of the horse's head and neck. Once the horse is walking positively forward the rider allows her legs to relax against the horse's sides. The arms and hands are drawn gently forward and back by the movement of the horse's head and neck. This movement is led by the horse. The rider does not pull back on the reins.

3 To prepare to return to the halt, the rider squeezes her legs inward against the horse's sides and at the same time reduces the degree to which she allows her arms to follow the movement of the horse's head and neck. On a well-schooled horse this very slight blocking of the free forward movement will be enough to halt the horse.

4 On a less responsive horse the rider will have to continue to reduce the degree to which the hands follow the horse's head and neck to the point where they are held still, which will completely block the forward movement. As soon as the horse halts, the rider should soften the hands as much as the horse will allow while still remaining at the halt. Until the horse halts, the rider's legs remain actively against the horse's sides, gently pushing him up into the hands. Once he has halted, the legs relax and remain gently in contact with his sides.

COMMON FAULTS

If the rider decides to do nothing with her legs and simply pulls on the reins in an effort to slow down, you can see what happens – the horse resists the request to slow down and throws his head and neck in the air in order to fight the pull of the rider; this is described as the horse hollowing against the rider. The whole picture looks tense and uncomfortable. The rider must first ask with the legs and then only use as much hand as is absolutely necessary to achieve the desired result.

this, you must be very quick to keep the soft forward movement of the hands. The horse may jump forward if he is tapped with the whip, and he must not then be punished by being pulled in the mouth. Remember to reward the horse for obeying and going forward. With practice, he will listen to you and a squeeze with your legs will be sufficient.

To halt the horse, squeeze with the legs but do not allow your hands to be drawn forward so much. The horse will realize that his forward movement is being blocked and will either slow down or

shorten the steps he is taking. Continue to decrease the forward movement of the hands until, if necessary, they are returned to the normal halt position and do not move forward at all. This complete blocking will halt the horse.

As with the leg aids, the long-term aim is to use as light and gentle an aid as possible. To begin with you may have to block completely with your hands but, with practice, the horse will become more attentive until only a slight reduction of the forward movement of the hands is enough to halt him.

CHANGING DIRECTION

You cannot continue in a straight line forever, so once you are confident with forward movement you must be able to change direction. When the legs are used together either on or fractionally behind the girth, and the hands are also moving together, the horse is kept in a straight line. To go around a corner, or to turn, the horse has to bend through his body. In order to achieve this, the hands and legs must be used individually. If one leg is allowed to slide further back behind the girth, this will make the horse move his hindquarters away from the leg in question, i.e. if your right leg is used behind the girth, the horse will be encouraged to move his quarters across to the left, and vice versa. So, to ask the horse to turn, the rider's inside leg is used on the girth, as you want him to bend his body around your leg as he makes the turn. The rider's outside leg is used behind the girth ready to stop the horse swinging his hindquarters out as he turns. The horse should never be turned sharply – any turn should be thought of as part of a circle, so to turn right think about circling away to the right. Then the right hand and leg are referred to as being on the inside, while the left hand and leg are now on the outside.

TURNING RIGHT

1 Horse and rider are about to turn off a straight line and away to the right. The rider has moved the right hand a few inches away from the withers, toward the right. This is called opening the hand, and it invites the horse to turn his head and neck to the right in preparation for the turn.

2 The rider's inside (right) leg is used on the girth to ask the horse to bend around it; the outside (left) leg is used behind the girth to prevent his quarters from swinging too far to the left. The left hand and arm soften so that the horse keeps bending to the right. The right hand stays to the right of the withers, inviting the horse to move that way.

3 As soon as the horse has turned as far around to the right as the rider requires, the hands and legs return to their normal position.

4 To turn right, the rider's inside (right) hand is moved a little to the right of the withers – opening the hand; the inside (right) leg remains on the girth, asking the horse to bend (turn) around it.

5 The outside hand is softened so that the horse can bend his head and neck away to the right, while the outside leg is used behind the girth to control the degree to which the hindquarters move.

TURNING LEFT

1 To turn left, the rider opens the inside (left) hand a few inches to the left to invite the horse to turn his head and neck in that direction. The left leg is used on the girth to ask the horse to bend (turn) around it.

2 The outside (right) hand is softened forward to allow the horse to turn away to the left, while the outside leg is used back behind the girth to control the swing of the hindquarters.

3 As soon as the horse is heading in the required direction, the rider's hands and legs return to the normal position.

4 To turn left, the inside (left) hand is opened out to the left to ask the horse to turn his head and neck to the left, while the inside leg is used on the girth.

5 The outside (right) hand must be allowed to soften forward to allow the horse to turn away to the left. The outside leg behind the girth controls the hind-quarters so that the horse's body is bent around the rider's inside leg.

▌ **RIGHT**
Riding forward
on a straight line.

▌ **FAR RIGHT**
Bending the horse so
that he can turn right.

rider's hands follow the
movement of the horse's
head and neck

rider's legs both used
on the girth to send
the horse forward

outside hand
controls the
degree to which
the horse's
head and neck
bend to the right

inside hand
opens outwards
to bend the
horse's head
and neck to
the right

outside leg
behind girth
bends the
horse's quarters
around inside leg

inside leg on
the girth – the
point around
which the
horse's body
must bend

FORWARD TO THE TROT

The trot is the next gait that the horse can offer you, and many new riders find this one of the hardest to master. When the horse trots, the rider feels a far more powerful force of movement from beneath than is experienced at walk. In order to feel comfortable with this gait, try to keep your body relaxed so that it absorbs the movement, rather than tensing up and being bounced around by the horse.

■ THE RISING TROT

When the horse trots you can either sit deep in the saddle the whole time – which is known as the sitting trot – or you can rise out of the saddle with each stride, in time with the beat of the trot. It is far less tiring – and more comfortable – for the new rider to learn the rising trot, than it is to master the sitting trot. Once you feel at ease at this pace, and are able to stay relaxed and balanced, then is the time to practise the sitting trot.

When the horse trots, he is springing from one diagonal pair of legs to the other. To rise to the trot, allow the spring from one pair of legs going forward to lift your seat out of the saddle. The seat returns to the saddle as the other pair of legs springs forward. So as the horse moves each pair of legs in a one-two, one-two, one-two beat, you are sitting and rising to the same beat: up-down, up-down, up-down. This movement of the rider is known as rising or posting.

THE TROT

The trot is a two-beat gait – the horse springs from one diagonal pair of legs to the other. If you listen to his hoofbeats, you only hear two footfalls within each complete stride. The outside hind and the inside foreleg move forward together; this is followed by a brief period of suspension, and then the inside hind and outside foreleg move forward as a pair.

THE RISING TROT

Mastering rising, or posting, to the trot takes time and practice, but it makes life much more comfortable to the horse and rider than sitting the whole time. Concentrate on keeping your upper body upright and allow the movement of the horse to help you rise out of the saddle, rather than actively pushing your body up and down. Keep your weight down in your heels and try to think of just letting your tummy be pushed forwards and up between your elbows. This will help prevent you tipping forwards and should help keep your hands low and still. Your hands do not rise with you – open and close your elbow joint to allow your body to rise while your hands stay still.

■ RISING ON THE CORRECT DIAGONAL

When riding at the rising trot on a circle, the rider is meant to rise in time with a particular diagonal pair of the horse's legs. The easiest way to explain what this entails is for you to look down and watch the horse's outside shoulder for a few minutes once you are trotting. You should be rising out of the saddle as the outside shoulder goes forward. As it comes back, you should sit again.

The reason for bothering to rise on the correct diagonal will become clear later when you are concerned with improving the quality of the horse's work. The horse will find it easier to balance himself on a turn or circle if the rider is in the saddle when the inside hind leg and the outside foreleg are touching the ground. As the horse uses his legs in diagonal pairs, this is achieved by sitting as the outside shoulder comes back, and rising as it goes forward. When you change the rein and circle in the opposite direction, it follows that you must also change the diagonal, i.e. rise as the new outside shoulder goes forward. Changing the diagonal is achieved by sitting for an extra beat before rising again. So instead of sit-rise, sit-rise, you would sit-rise, sit-sit-rise and this will put you on the correct diagonal.

At the sitting trot the rider retains the correct classical position, allowing her stomach and lower back to absorb the movement of the horse. Note the straight line through the shoulder, hip and heel, as well as the line from the elbow, down along the rein to the bit.

COMMON FAULTS

A common mistake made at the rising trot is actively trying to push the body up and down. This causes the shoulders and arms to bob up and down, which is disconcerting and uncomfortable for the horse since his mouth suffers if there is excessive movement of the hands and arms.

Another common mistake at the rising trot is for the rider's shoulders to tip forward. This puts the rider off balance and means the hands are often rested on the horse's neck in an effort to regain balance. If the hands are resting on the neck, they cannot keep a soft but continuous contact with the horse's mouth. The shoulders must stay upright, just as they do when the rider is stationary; only the hips should move forward. If the shoulders remain balanced and in line with the rider's heels, the rider will not be pushed off balance by the movement of the horse.

■ THE SITTING TROT

At the sitting trot you should remain sitting deep in the saddle, maintaining the same classical position as when stationary and at the walk. The movement of the horse is absorbed by the stomach and lower back, so that you remain deep in the saddle without being bounced up and down. As you feel the horse's legs springing forward underneath you, try to think of allowing your ribcage to sink down toward your hips. This means that the stomach and lower back act like an accordion: As the horse springs along at the trot, the stomach and lower back are either contracting or expanding to absorb the movement. You must stay relaxed so that your legs can hang long and loose by the horse's sides, and your arms can still stay soft and maintain a light contact with the horse's mouth. It helps to make a conscious effort to keep breathing – you would be surprised how many riders hold their breath as soon as they concentrate too hard on something. Steady breathing helps you relax.

At the sitting trot, the rider's knee joint should be kept as long and loose as possible.

A common fault is to grip with and tighten up the knee. This will make it even harder to sit to the movement of the horse.

COMMON FAULTS AT THE SITTING TROT

▌ LEFT
Back to the armchair position! How not
to sit – the lower leg has slipped forward
and the rider is now sitting on the back
of her seat. The line from the shoulder
through the hip to the heel has been lost.

▌ LEFT
If you fall into the armchair position your
body is unable correctly to absorb the
movement of the horse. You will be
bumped up and down and, as a result, you
will find your hands and arms bobbing up
and down as well. It's uncomfortable for
both horse and rider.

FROM WALK TO TROT TO WALK

1 The horse should be walking forward actively and attentively before the rider asks for the trot. See how the rider is keeping a contact with the horse's mouth without actually pulling or restricting him. The rider's legs are in contact with the horse's sides but are not being used actively. By keeping both the legs and the hands in contact with the horse in this way, you will be keeping open your lines of communication.

2 To ask for the trot, the rider squeezes both legs actively against the horse's sides and softens the hands forward so that the horse feels free to increase the pace and go forward into the trot.

3 Once the horse is trotting, the rider's legs and hands return to just being in contact with the horse. The leg is there to squeeze the horse forward should he slow down, and the hand is there to guide him.

4 To return to the walk the rider sits deep in the saddle and squeezes the legs against the horse's sides. (If the rider had been at the rising trot, she would return to the sitting trot to achieve this.)

5 Then, instead of softening the hands forward, she keeps the hands still so that the horse's forward movement is blocked, bringing him back to the walk.

6 As soon as the horse walks, the hands and legs relax sufficiently to keep just a light contact.

ON INTO THE CANTER

It is at the canter that the new rider will first experience the true exhilaration of riding a horse. The feeling of speed and power as the horse eats up the ground with each stride gives a real buzz. Despite the increased speed, the rider generally finds this a very smooth gait.

■ CANTERING ON THE CORRECT LEAD

If you watch a horse cantering in a circle, he should appear to be leading each stride with his inside foreleg. In practice, the inside foreleg is actually the last leg to be moved by the horse within each canter stride, but to the observer it does appear

■ LEFT
At the canter, the rider sits deeply in the saddle and allows the hips to be rocked forward and back by the movement of the horse. The arms and hands must stay soft and relaxed so that they can follow the movement of the horse's head and neck. Note once more the straight line through the ear, shoulder, hip and heel, and again from the elbow, down the rein to the bit. At all gaits, the correct classical position should be maintained.

THE CANTER

The canter is a three-time pace, with the legs working in the following sequence: outside hind goes forward, then the inside hind and outside fore go forward together, followed by the inside foreleg. There is then a period of suspension when all four feet are off the ground, before the stride pattern is repeated – outside hind, inside hind and outside fore together, then inside fore.

to be leading the stride. When this is the case, the horse is said to be cantering on the correct leg, or the correct lead. So when cantering on the right rein, i.e. circling to the right, the inside (right) foreleg should appear to be leading; and, when cantering on the left rein, the inside (left) foreleg appears to be leading.

To ask the horse to canter forward on the left lead you should use the inside leg on the girth and the outside leg behind the girth, while opening the left hand slightly to keep the horse bent left, and just keeping a feel on the outside rein to stop the horse from simply accelerating at the trot. To canter on the right lead the aids are reversed; the right leg is used on the girth, the left leg is used behind the girth, and the right hand is opened slightly to bend the horse to the right.

Cantering on the correct lead. This horse and rider are circling on the left rein and you can see how the horse's inside (left) foreleg appears to be leading.

Cantering on the wrong lead. Here you can see that, although the horse is still circling to the left, it is the outside foreleg that appears to be leading the stride.

FROM TROT TO CANTER TO TROT

1 Before asking the horse to canter, the rider must go into sitting trot and be sure that the horse is working forward actively and attentively at the trot.

2 To ask the horse to go forward into a canter on the left rein, i.e. to canter on the left lead, the rider sits deep, presses the inside (left) leg on the girth, but asks more actively with a squeeze or a nudge of the outside leg back behind the girth. This is because it is the horse's outside hindleg that starts off the stride, so the rider activates this leg by using her own outside leg behind the girth. The inside hand is opened out slightly to the left to encourage the horse to keep a bend to the left, but the outside hand may have to keep more of a feel than usual on the outside rein to prevent the horse from simply trotting faster. In this picture the outside hind is just about to take the first step of the canter stride.

3 Once the correct canter is established, with the left leg leading, the rider just keeps her outside leg in place behind the girth to encourage the outside hind to keep initiating the canter stride. The inside leg remains at the girth, so that the horse's body is bent around the rider's inside leg as they progress around the circle.

4 The arms and hands move forward with the movement of the horse's head and neck, and the rider sits deep in the saddle, allowing her hips to be rocked by the horse's stride.

5 In order to return to the trot the rider sits deep in the saddle and closes both legs against the horse's sides.

6 The rider reduces the degree to which she allows her hands and arms to move forward with the horse's head and neck, so that the horse's forward movement is blocked. You may have to keep a slightly stronger feel in the outside hand to help bring the horse back to the trot.

7 As soon as the trot is established the rider softens her hands forward again to follow the movement and allows her legs to hang softly by the horse's sides. She must be ready to squeeze the horse forward again into a more active trot if he tries to slow down any more.

COMMON FAULT

A common fault when asking the horse to canter is for the rider to tip forward and look down over the inside shoulder. As soon as the rider's shoulders drop forward she is pushed off balance, and then the hands tend to drop down on to the horse looking for support. The rider must stay sitting upright and use her hands and legs independently to ask for a transition to the canter. Leaning forward simply unbalances both horse and rider, and this makes the job harder.

CANTERING IN THE FORWARD SEAT

By taking his weight out of the saddle, the rider can encourage the horse to relax his back and put a little more life and swing into his canter. This is often done out on a hack so that the horse is allowed to move along effortlessly under his rider. In a schooling session, the rider may take his weight out of the saddle to help the horse relax and use his back more. This is often done when the horse is being warmed up before he is asked to jump. It is called riding in the forward seat, and the rider simply lifts his seat bones out of the saddle and allows his weight to sink down into his heels and the stirrups. The rider will need to have gained a good sense of balance to do this, and will also need quite strong leg muscles, as it really stretches the backs of the calves. If you feel you keep leaning back in the saddle, you probably need to bring your shoulders slightly more forward. If you feel you are leaning forward on to the horse's neck, you need to raise your shoulders and check that your lower leg has not slipped backward, which will in turn push your weight forward.

FULL SPEED AHEAD – THE GALLOP

Riding your horse at the gallop is an invigorating and exciting experience, but for it to be safe and enjoyable for both horse and rider you must develop a well-balanced, secure seat and feel confident about controlling your horse. Balance and security are important because if you lose

THE GALLOP

The gallop is a four-time gait with the legs working in the following sequence: near hind, off hind, near fore, off fore. Because the walk is also a four-time gait it is often said that if a horse has a good walk he will also be a good galloper. Watch race horses walking around at the track and you will appreciate this!

At gallop the horse is at full stretch – he lengthens out his body and neck, and each leg is fully extended as it powers forward over the ground. The rider tucks her upper body in behind the horse's neck so that the outline of the two is as streamlined as possible. The seat is taken out of the saddle, which means the rider's weight is dropped down into the heel and is also pushed further back to allow the rider's upper body to tuck in behind the horse's neck. The rider's arms extend forward as the horse stretches his neck forward within each stride. It is usual to ride with shorter stirrups when galloping, as this makes it easier for the rider's weight to be lifted out of the saddle. The lower leg remains on the girth unless the stirrups are pulled up very short, in which case the lower leg is usually pushed forward in front of the girth with the weight well down in the heel, as demonstrated by any race rider.

your balance at this gait you will either topple off, or end up hanging on to the reins. The horse will fight this pressure on his mouth, and you may find yourself no longer in control. At this pace the horse is at full stretch and, to allow him to use himself fully, you should bring your weight up out of the saddle, push your seat further back and tuck your upper body in behind the horse's neck, very much like a race jockey but without quite such short stirrups.

HIGH SPIRITS

Most horses enjoy a good gallop and will quite often let their riders know this by popping in a high-spirited leap or buck. If the rider is able to sit this out, it is no more than clean, harmless fun, but it becomes less amusing when it is sufficient to unseat the rider. When cantering or galloping, always keep a contact through the reins with the horse's mouth in order to help balance him. If the horse becomes playful and over-excited in his work, it is even more important to maintain this contact.

STOPPING A HARD-PULLING HORSE

It is often at the faster paces, canter and gallop, that the horse becomes over-excited to the extent that he is less responsive to his rider, particularly when it comes to slowing down again. While in theory it should be possible to stop a horse at any pace by using the subtle balance of hand and leg, in practice the horse's excitement can override his desire to listen to his rider. If you find yourself struggling to slow down a galloping horse, make sure your lower leg is pushed forward while still squeezing both legs against the horse's sides. The slightly forward lower leg position allows you to brace yourself against the stirrup. When a horse gets strong, it is easy to be pulled forward out of the saddle; the lower leg slips back putting the rider in a very vulnerable position. Shorten up the reins as much as you can and put one hand, still holding the rein, tight into the horse's neck. Use the other hand

to keep a strong hold on the other rein and, by gradually giving and taking this rein, the horse will start to listen again and will slow down. If you keep a continuous pull on the rein, the horse will simply lean on the bit and become stronger still – give and take the rein to prevent him doing this. Circling the horse will also cause him to slow down.

INFLUENCING THE HORSE

There is a subtle difference between learning to ride and actually influencing the horse. The new rider will spend the early period of training simply learning how to sit correctly balanced on the horse, and mastering the basic aids which will enable horse and rider to proceed at the walk, trot and canter, to halt and to circle left or right. Until you achieve this balance and the resulting independent seat, you will be little more than a passenger on the horse. Once you have acquired an independent seat, you can concern yourself with how well or otherwise your horse is performing underneath you. Riding a horse should be a pleasure for both parties – the ultimate aim is to be mounted on a co-operative horse who will respond to your lightest instruction. When this is achieved, those observing you may well marvel at that closest of secrets – the one between a rider and his horse.

CONTROL OF THE HORSE

Use your hands and legs to control and influence the horse's shoulders, hindquarters, head and neck. When making a turn or circling, the horse's shoulders and hindquarters are controlled by the rider's use of the legs. When combined with the hands, this can be taken further still to move the horse in a number of different ways. The rider's leg can be used behind the girth to encourage the horse to move sideways (laterally) away from the leg, or to control the swing and direction of the quarters. The use of the leg at the girth encourages the horse to bend around the leg and allows the rider to control the horse's shoulder.

MOVING THE HINDQUARTERS TO THE LEFT

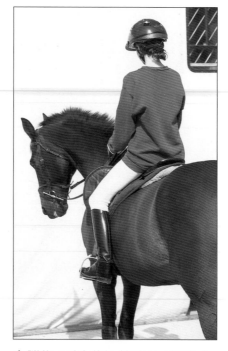

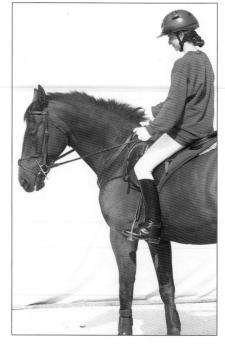

1 While at a halt, if the rider keeps a light feel on the outside rein (the right rein), opens out the inside rein a few inches and squeezes the horse's side with her inside leg at the girth while the outside leg remains relaxed, the horse will bend his head and neck to the left.

2 If the rider presses her inside (left) leg against the horse's side and continues to ask for some left bend with the inside hand, but prevents the horse from moving forwards by blocking with the outside hand, the horse will step sideways to the right. The rider should think of pushing the horse from the inside leg over on to the outside rein. The outside leg and hand then control how far you allow the horse to step to the right. Mastering these combinations of hand and leg aids will allow you to learn how to move your horse's body in many different ways. This control is then used in different schooling exercises to help the horse become more supple and responsive for whatever job you want him to do.

MOVING THE HINDQUARTERS TO THE RIGHT

1 Similarly at a halt, if the rider keeps a light feel on the outside (left) rein and opens the inside hand while pressing the inside leg against the girth, the horse will bend his head and neck to the right.

2 If the rider brings her outside (left) leg back behind the girth while blocking any attempt by the horse to move forward with the outside rein, and keeps her inside (right) leg on the girth to keep the horse's shoulders stationary, then as she presses her outside leg against the horse he will swing his quarters over to the right. To straighten the horse up again the aids are then reversed – the right leg is used behind the girth to push the quarters back over to the left, while the right hand prevents the horse from stepping forward. The left leg is used at the girth to make sure the shoulders remain still. Once the horse is straight again, the rider's legs and hands return to the normal position.

THE RIDER'S GOAL –
TO LIGHTEN THE FOREHAND

If you watch a horse showing off loose in a field you will see how proud and active he can look: His neck is high and arched, and he will use his hindquarters powerfully to produce round, elevated strides. As soon as a young or unschooled horse is asked to carry a rider, this picture can change dramatically: the horse's outline becomes flatter and longer, his steps lose their spring and he may lean on the bit by carrying his head and neck low, so that the rider always has a horrible, heavy feel in the hand; alternatively, he may carry his head high in an effort to evade the effect of the rider's hand on the rein and the bit. The rider has to teach the horse how to rebalance himself so that he can comfortably deal with the unbalancing effect of a rider on his back and regain his proud, elegant and light bearing.

An unbalanced horse usually takes advantage of the fact that the rider is holding the reins and will lean on the bit, so the rider is in effect helping to carry the weight of the horse. When this happens the horse is said to be on his forehand, i.e. more of the combined weight of the horse and the rider is carried on the horse's shoulders and forelegs than on the hindquarters and hind legs. If you piled a lot of heavy weights on to the front of a car it would become heavy to handle, and similarly the horse becomes heavy in the rider's hand and is difficult to steer and control. If the weight is taken off the front of the car and loaded on to the back, suddenly the car is light and maneuverable in front.

The rider's aim is to encourage the horse to carry more of the weight on the hindquarters than on the forehand. In order to do this the horse has to lower his hindquarters and allow his hind legs to step much further under his body. When he does this, his shoulders, head and neck are automatically raised. This is called lightening the forehand, or transferring the weight from the forehand to the hindquarters.

ENGAGING THE HINDQUARTERS

1 This horse is being worked in a long, low outline. A young horse will be worked like this until he builds up enough strength and balance to then be asked by the rider to start to carry more of his weight on his hindquarters, and to lighten his forehand.

2 The rider has used her legs and seat to encourage the horse to bring his hind legs further underneath him, and just keeps enough contact on the rein to keep the horse from speeding up. The effect of the rider's legs pushing the horse up into the contact maintained by the hand is that the horse starts to bend and flex his hocks more, so that they can step further underneath the body. This is called engaging the hocks or hindquarters.

3 Various schooling exercises, combined with the horse learning to become more responsive to the leg and seat aids, gradually allow the rider to encourage the horse to use his hindquarters more.

4 The horse's outline is now rounder, and the forehand has been raised slightly higher than the hindquarters so that the horse is carrying more of the weight on the hindquarters and has lightened the forehand. Asking the horse to transfer the weight in this way, from the forehand to the hindquarters, is always brought about by greater use of the rider's legs, not by pulling the horse's head and neck up and in with the reins. The rein contact should remain soft and elastic, only blocking sufficiently to prevent the horse from speeding up when the leg is applied, instead of engaging the hindquarters more as is required.

CONTROL AND MOTION – INTRODUCING LATERAL WORK

When first learning to ride, you are concerned primarily with being able to send the horse forward into the walk, trot, canter and gallop, and being able to halt. As your skills develop, you learn how to make the horse move sideways, either by moving his whole body or just his shoulders or hindquarters. This is known as lateral work, and is invaluable for a rider as it teaches him or her to feel and influence the horse's movement. For the horse, it is used as a suppling exercise and to encourage him to work more actively with his hindquarters.

LEG YIELDING

Lateral movements include leg yielding, haunches-in (both described here), shoulder-in and half-pass (see Developing Lateral Work). All horses should be introduced to these exercises as part of their overall training programme. Practise them at the walk and, once you have mastered control of the shoulders and hindquarters, you will realize just how manoeuvrable the horse can be.

■ **LEG YIELDING**
In this exercise the horse is asked to move forward and sideways at the same time;

the inside hind and foreleg cross over in front of the outside hind and foreleg.

■ **HAUNCHES-IN**
In this exercise the horse continues walking in a straight line but he brings his hind end in to one side. If working on a sand surface, the horse's hoofprints would leave three lines of tracks: the inside line is formed by the inside hind, the middle line is made by the inside fore and the outside hind (which follow each other), and the outside line is made by the outside fore.

■ **REIN BACK**
The rein back is when the horse is asked, quite literally, to walk backward. It should only ever be performed at the walk, although when frightened, the horse will be quite capable of running backward at a respectable speed!

Although the rein back is not a lateral movement, it is all part of teaching horse and rider the full extent of the control and motion they can achieve.

The horse should step backward, in a straight line, moving his legs clearly and positively in diagonal pairs – inside fore and outside hind together, followed by outside fore and inside hind together.

▌ **LEFT**
In leg yield, the horse maintains a bend throughout his body while stepping forwards and sideways at the same time. To leg yield to the left, as shown here, the rider asks for right bend by pressing her right leg on to the girth, and opening her right hand slightly. Then think of pushing the horse from your right leg over on to your left hand. The left hand can be carried a little to the left to invite the horse to step to the left, and also dictates the speed and the degree of sideways movement. The outside leg is placed behind the girth to control the hindquarters as the horse steps across. The angle of the leg yield can be shallow or acute, depending on how the rider uses the combination of hand and leg.

HAUNCHES-IN

▌ RIGHT

In these pictures the horse is being asked to bring his hindquarters to the left while continuing to walk forward in a straight line. The rider uses her outside (right) leg behind the girth to move the quarters across slightly. Her inside leg stays on the girth to encourage the horse to keep moving forward and to prevent the shoulders from moving out of line. The left hand is opened slightly which, combined with the pressure from the left leg on the girth, encourages the horse to keep a bend through his whole body. The outside hand takes up enough of a feel to keep the horse's shoulder moving forward in a straight line.

Haunches-in to the right is achieved by reversing the aids – the left leg is used behind the girth, etc.

REIN BACK

1 The rein back can only be successfully performed if the horse is calm and relaxed when at the halt.

2 The rider squeezes both legs against the horse's sides, but makes sure that she blocks the horse's forward movement by not allowing her hands to move forward. Because the legs are applied actively, the horse knows he has to move somewhere. The rein contact is telling him he cannot go forward and so he goes backward. Some horses, as demonstrated here, understand what is required more easily if you apply both legs behind the girth, and then lift your seat bones off the saddle. This encourages the horse to step back underneath you as required.

3 Having taken one step back with one diagonal pair of legs, the horse proceeds to step back with the remaining diagonal pair. The horse should only be asked to step backward for a limited number of steps. As a reward, allow him to walk forward again while making a fuss over him.

ACCEPTANCE OF CONTACT

Right from the start the horse has to learn to accept, without tension or resentment, the fact that the bit in his mouth is attached, via the reins, to the rider's hands, and that there will always be a light but sympathetic contact between the two. It is vital that you achieve a balanced, independent seat so that you are not tempted to hang on to the reins in an effort to balance yourself. Your priority is to learn to follow the movement of the horse's head and neck so that you are able to keep a constant but sympathetic contact with his mouth. In the early stages of training, you should not concern yourself with how the horse is carrying his head and neck, but only with learning to feel,

BASIC PRINCIPLES

Before you can hope to achieve a lightening of the forehand, there are a number of basic principles that you and your horse must master. These form the basis of all horses' training and progression, whether or not you are dealing with a horse who has never been properly schooled, and are as follows:
- Acceptance of the rein contact.
- Free forward movement.
- Maintaining a rhythm.
- Bend and flexion through the body.
- The use of half-halts to engage the hindquarters and rebalance the horse.
Once you have mastered these principles, you will be equipped with the means to ride your horse to the maximum of his potential.

follow and maintain the contact. Once the horse knows that the contact is constant, but kind, he will learn to accept it. Your elbows must remain soft and relaxed so that the contact can be maintained. It may be necessary to open the hands out a little wider than usual so that there is no obstruction – whatever the horse does with his head, you can follow it with your hands.

FOLLOWING THE HORSE'S HEAD AND NECK

▮ RIGHT
In the early stages of training, the rider should not concern herself with the position of the horse's head and neck – only with learning to follow their movement so that a soft but constant contact is maintained. Try to think of the contact as something that is alive, rather than as something static. The feel down the rein will fluctuate constantly with the changing movement and balance of the horse. The rider must maintain a consistent contact whatever the horse does with his head and neck, otherwise the horse will learn that if he snatches the reins or throws his head around, he can escape the contact. He has to understand that the contact is always going to be there, but it needs to be sympathetic and elastic so that the horse is confident to move forwards into it.

Ultimately the aim is to have an even feel in both reins, but the horse doesn't necessarily offer this automatically! Think of your hands being a pair of scales and the contact is a weight in each one. If one hand feels heavier then use your leg on the heavy side to push the horse into the lighter hand so that the scales are balanced.

COMMON FAULTS

How often have you seen a horse dragging along like this? The rider is not keeping a contact with the horse's mouth and, although she is actively using her legs, the horse is completely ignoring the aid and continuing to plod along in a lethargic and disinterested manner.

The horse must respond the same way at all gaits. Here, at the trot, we can see the result of the rider failing to keep a contact with the horse's mouth, and the horse blatantly ignoring the rider's leg aids. The rider is working hard with her legs while the horse is being extremely lazy with his!

FREE FORWARD MOVEMENT

The horse also has to learn to respect the rider's legs, i.e. when you use your legs against the horse's sides, he must respond by going forward if both legs are used together or by moving away from the leg if used as a lateral (sideways) aid. The vast majority of problems experienced both on the flat and over jumps are caused by the horse ignoring, or being slow to react to, the rider's leg aids. The horse's first reaction should always be to move forward. Once the horse respects the leg and is willing to maintain free forward movement without you continually having to reapply the leg aids, he is said to be in front of the leg and on the aids – he is attentive and ready to react to his rider's commands instantly.

In the early stages of training, you should use your voice combined with a squeeze from both legs to ask the horse to move forward. If the horse does not respond, use your voice again, backed up with a sharp nudge with both heels against the horse's sides. If this is still ignored, squeeze your legs against the horse, use your voice to ask him to walk on and give him a tap with the schooling whip or stick behind your leg at the same time as the leg aid is applied. You must be ready to allow forward movement with the hands, particularly if the horse jumps forward when the schooling whip is used. As soon as he moves forward, reward him by praising him verbally. You should then relax your legs against the horse's sides. As soon as he slows down again, repeat the process. Gradually the horse will learn to respond to the first light aid.

KEEPING A SOFT CONTACT

1 Here the rider has shortened her reins sufficiently to keep a contact with the horse's mouth. She has applied the leg again and backed it up with a tap from the schooling whip. Already the picture is one of greater alertness and activity.

2 The rider maintains the contact and uses the leg once more to ask the horse to walk on a little more energetically.

3 This time the horse responds instantly; the rider's leg can relax and the horse maintains the forward movement without further nagging. Note how the horse's outline is now much rounder and shorter as he begins to lighten his forehand.

4 At the trot, the rider takes up contact with the horse's mouth and backs up her leg aids with a tap from the schooling whip.

5 Immediately the horse offers much more in the way of forward impulsion. Now that he is thinking forward, see how he lengthens his steps and voluntarily raises his head and neck into a rounder, shorter outline.

6 The rider can relax her legs and enjoy the free forward movement that the horse is offering her. But as soon as he drops back from this pace, the rider starts the process over again.

MAINTAINING A RHYTHM

Now that the horse accepts the contact and moves forward willingly from your leg, both you and he need to learn to maintain an even rhythm in all your work. This rhythm must not be too slow or the work will lack impulsion and power; also, it must not be too fast or the horse will tend to become unbalanced and will be pushed on to his forehand. Aim for a rhythm at each gait that gives you the feeling of free forward movement without feeling rushed. The ultimate aim is to use a light squeeze from the legs to ride the horse up into this rhythm; then to relax and enjoy the experience while the horse willingly maintains the rhythm, without continual nagging from either hand or leg.

Once the horse is responding quickly to the leg you are halfway there. Some horses have naturally rhythmic gaits and will automatically maintain the rhythm. Others will need a reminder from leg, voice and/or schooling whip to keep up to the rhythm, or they may need to be slowed down. Once the horse is thinking forward, be careful not to dampen his goodwill by restricting him with the reins if he goes too fast. The use of a neck strap to slow the horse is a better method to use; it prevents the horse from learning how to lean on the bit or to fight you by shortening and tensing his neck.

By pulling on the neck strap instead of blocking with the reins, you can slow the horse down. Practise in the arena, first using the strap to bring the horse from walk to halt, and then from trot to walk etc. Once the horse understands its use, this method can be used to steady him within any pace. But remember that you must still use your legs and voice, if necessary, in the same way you would if you were going to use the rein contact to slow down.

USING THE NECK STRAP

1 Here the rider is introducing the neck strap by using it to bring the horse back from trot to walk. She has put the reins in one hand and holds the neck strap in the other.

2 The rider then uses her legs with a light squeeze against the horse's sides, while using her voice and a firm pull on the neck strap to slow the horse down. Although the rider wants to slow down, the leg is still applied because it encourages the horse to bring his hindlegs further underneath him so that he can keep his forehand light. If the leg is not used, the horse will simply shift his weight on to the forehand and will become heavy and unbalanced in the rider's hand.

3 The horse comes back quite happily to the walk without the need to block with the rein. He is rewarded with a pat and praise from his rider. With a forward-thinking horse, the neck strap allows you to encourage him to maintain a steady rhythm without having to first resort to taking a stronger contact on the reins. This stronger contact can sometimes cause the horse to shorten and tighten his neck and fight against the bit – the neck strap is a better way of helping him understand what you want him to do, whilst keeping his neck and mouth relaxed.

4 When working at the trot, if the horse has a tendency to speed up out of the desired rhythm, the rider can just loop a finger through the neck strap and pull on it until the horse slows the rhythm down again.

5 When the horse responds, the neck strap is released and he is praised by his rider.

BEND AND FLEXION

In all the horse's work, the rider is striving to ensure that the horse's hindlegs follow in the same tracks as his front legs, i.e. his quarters are not allowed to swing out or his shoulder to fall in. This is referred to as straightness in the horse, which is a term that causes some confusion. For the horse to be straight, i.e. for his hindlegs to follow in the same tracks as his front legs, when working on a turn or a circle he has to bend through his body; his whole body must form a slight, continual curve around the rider's inside leg. So in order to be straight the horse has to bend!

The degree of bend that the horse shows through his body is dependent on the size of circle or turn you are riding. For example, to ride a 65½ foot (20 m) circle the horse shows only a slight bend through his body, but to manoeuvre himself around a 33 foot (10 m) circle there will be a greater degree of bend.

BELOW
The horse is bringing his hocks well underneath himself, the hindquarters are lowered slightly and the poll and jaw are relaxed so that the front of the face is on the vertical.

ACHIEVING BEND

1 To achieve the correct bend through the horse's body, the rider needs to think about pushing the horse from the inside leg on to her outside hand. The horse needs to bend his body (like a banana!) around the rider's inside leg. So apply the inside leg firmly on to the girth and bring the inside hand a little to the right (open the inside hand) to invite the horse to bend that way. The energy created by the rider's legs is then felt and contained in the outside hand. The outside hand has to allow the horse to continue to travel forwards while controlling the degree to which you want the horse to bend. If the outside hand gives too much, the horse will just bend his neck to the right rather than bend his whole body around the rider's inside leg.

2 The rider should now feel the horse bending through the body and neck; if the horse resists and does not respond by offering some bend through his body, the rider simply applies more pressure on the contact with the inside hand by opening it out wider, while controlling the neck and outside shoulder with the outside hand. By using an open inside hand, you avoid the common problem of shortening and tightening the horse's neck. The inside leg is kept on, and should be backed up with a tap from the schooling whip if the horse continues to fall in on the circle rather than bend through the body. The outside leg will be placed behind the girth to prevent the horse swinging his quarters to the outside.

3 As soon as the horse offers the bend, i.e. when you can see a glimpse of his inside eye and nostril, use both legs against his sides to encourage him to bring his hocks further underneath him and to flex through his topline. When you feel the horse relax his poll and jaw so that the nose is lowered and his face is on the vertical, soften the inside rein and allow it to follow the movement in the same way as the outside rein. Praise the horse verbally – this is his reward for yielding to your leg and hand. The horse is now beginning to work in self-carriage, i.e. he is carrying more weight on his hindquarters and is lightening his forehand. Note that his head and neck are higher and more arched than in picture one; this is a result of the hocks being brought further under him.

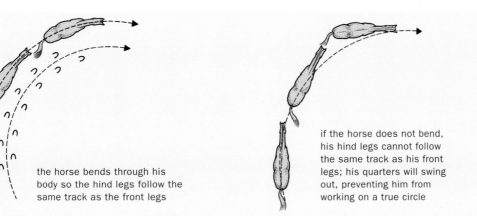

the horse bends through his body so the hind legs follow the same track as the front legs

if the horse does not bend, his hind legs cannot follow the same track as his front legs; his quarters will swing out, preventing him from working on a true circle

▮ **LEFT**
How a horse goes around a corner.

The more the horse has to bend his body, the more he has to use his hocks, and the inside hind leg in particular has to step much further under the horse's body in order to follow in the track of the inside foreleg. Having ridden simple turns and circles, you will know that the inside leg is used at the girth with an open inside hand to encourage the horse to bend around the inside leg, while the outside leg is used back behind the girth to prevent the quarters from swinging out. The outside hand is used to prevent the horse from bending his head and neck too much to the inside. On an unschooled horse the aids have to be exaggerated until he realizes what it is you are asking him to do. Once the horse is willing to offer you the bend through his whole body, you can ask him to flex right through his topline so that his whole outline becomes soft and round and he offers you no resistance whatsoever. The horse's topline describes the area from the top of the tail, over the hindquarters, back, withers and neck, and on up to the poll. When the horse flexes through his topline, his hindquarters are lowered as his hocks come further underneath him, he stays soft through his back, arches his neck and relaxes his poll and jaw so that the head is carried in a relaxed manner; the horse will lower his nose so that a vertical line could be drawn down the front of his face.

The horse should be introduced to this work at the trot – it is very easy to stifle his forward momentum if it is first asked for at the walk. Ride forward into the trot, bearing in mind the principles of having a horse who will respond happily to your leg and settle into a rhythm without being nagged by your leg or hand.

With time and practice, you will find that the horse will become more and more responsive to the request to bend and flex. After a while, you will not need to open the inside hand in such an exaggerated fashion; simply moving the hand over

OBTAINING THE CORRECT DEGREE OF BEND

The rider should only ask for a slight bend through the horse's body and neck, so that the outside of the horse makes a continual curve around the rider's inside leg. The rider only needs to see a glimpse of the horse's inside eye and nostril to know that the bend is correct.

A common fault is for the horse to bend only through the neck from the withers, so that his body is still straight. In this position the horse can avoid having to step under himself more with his hind legs, so his quarters will swing out as he goes around a corner. If his hocks are not underneath him, he can neither turn correctly nor flex through his topline when asked. The rider must use the outside rein to reduce the degree of bend in the neck, the outside leg to keep the hind-quarters from swinging out, and should reinforce the inside leg by tapping the horse with the schooling whip behind his or her lower leg.

Another fault is for the horse to tilt his head toward the inside. He is allowing the rider's inside hand to draw his nose to the inside but is ignoring the outside hand, so instead of bending through the neck and poll, the horse simply tilts his head to one side. More contact should be taken up with the outside rein to correct this.

BEND AND FLEXION – THE OVERALL PICTURE

1 The horse is ridden forward at the trot; the rider opens her inside hand and closes her inside leg on the girth to ask the horse to bend around her leg. The outside hand stays soft and allows the horse to move freely forward, unless it has to be used to prevent him bending too much through the neck.

2 Here the horse has responded by curving his whole body around the rider's inside leg; see how the neck looks more relaxed and softer than in the first picture. This is because the horse is working willingly, without resistance.

3 Now that the rider has obtained the correct amount of bend, she closes both legs against the horse's sides to encourage him to be more active and step further under himself with his hind legs. The horse is now flexing through his topline, i.e. his quarters are lowered and his back and neck are round and soft, which in turn raises and lightens his forehand.

4 The result is a picture of power with softness, and roundness with activity. See how the horse is bent around the rider's legs; he is also using his hind-quarters actively, which allows his forehand to be light and elevated. The increased power shows in the way the horse is stretching his front legs forward, and matching this up behind by stepping under himself further with the hind-legs. His neck is carried higher and is more arched than in the first picture but he remains soft and light in the rider's hand. This is the start of self-carriage.

about an inch will be sufficient. Much further down the line in the horse's training, it will also only be necessary to take up a feel on the inside rein and to close the legs against the horse's sides to achieve bend and flexion.

Once the bend and flexion are established at the trot, you can strive for the same result at both the walk and the canter. The vital thing to remember with this training method is always to reward the horse by softening the inside hand the instant that he offers you even the tiniest degree of flexion and relaxation. To begin with it will be a case of working quite hard to ask the horse to bend and then to flex, followed by the reward of softening the inside hand as soon as he does so. He may only offer you the bend and flexion for a few strides before you have to repeat the

process and ask again, but as he begins to understand what is wanted and his topline muscles up as a result of the work, he will offer it to you for longer periods.

Gradually you will be doing less asking and more rewarding; you will find yourself riding for longer with both hands soft so that the horse is working on a light contact. But you will need to be persistent and consistent in your training.

This horse has offered the rider the required degree of bend and flexion – note the arch of his neck and how his forehand appears lighter and higher than his hindquarters. You can see how he is really flexing his hock as he goes to step forward with his hind leg and, most importantly, note how the rider has softened the inside rein so that the horse is holding this outline himself.

■ RIGHT
As soon as the horse responds to the rider's aids by bending through his body and then flexing through his topline, the rider must soften the inside hand and praise the horse verbally as a reward. This is the only way that the horse can know that he has responded to the aids in the right way.

■ RIGHT
While the inside hand is being softened, it can also be used to pat the horse's neck as further praise.

CORRECT USE OF THE INSIDE HAND

It is vital to ask the horse to bend his whole body around your inside leg by opening the inside hand and using the inside leg to keep the horse out on the circle. By using your hand and leg in this way, when the horse does respond he will produce a continuous bend through his body, neck and head. You may have to open your inside hand very wide, you may have to back up the inside-leg aid with a tap from the schooling whip, and your outside hand may have to take up more of a contact to keep the horse from bending his neck too far to the inside, but, when the horse drops his resistance, relaxes and responds to these aids, he will be working correctly.

If the horse is slow to respond and refuses to offer the requested bend, it is very tempting to cheat! If you cross your inside hand over the horse's withers instead of opening the hand out and backing it up with the inside leg, the horse will instantly bend, but this bend will only be from the withers. It will not be right through the body. The crossing over of the rider's hand cuts off the horse's forward impulsion and cuts off the bend at the withers. So while you will be able to see the required glimpse of the inside eye and nostril, it will not be backed up by the correct use or position of the horse's hindquarters.

Crossing the inside hand over in this way is something that many riders, even at high levels

of competition, are tempted to do. Some do not realize that it is a false measure and are satisfied with the false bend that the horse offers them, but their future is limited and their potential will not be fully realized. The temptation to cross the hand over is simply a sign that the horse is not respecting the rider's inside leg and/or the outside hand. So instead of giving in to the temptation, use it as a reminder to yourself to use your inside leg and outside hand correctly, even if this means not

continuing with the exercise until the horse is prepared to move away from the inside leg (see Free Forward Movement). Always go back and correct the underlying fault if any training exercise is not progressing well. Never think that a short cut such as crossing the hand over or losing your temper will pay long-term dividends. Get the basics right and then you will have something permanent to build on. Be consistent, and be quick to praise your horse.

When asking the horse to bend, you must open your inside hand and use your inside leg.

If you cross your inside hand over, the horse will bend only from the wither.

WORKING
WITHIN EACH
GAIT

Once both horse and rider have begun to understand the
basics of a correct and acceptable way of working at each
gait, the rider can take the horse's performance further.
Having mastered the principles of free forward
movement and obtained a degree of bend and flexion,
you can further influence the horse by seeking to
improve his gaits. Plenty of horses have a pleasant
enough way of going – they are able to maintain a round
outline and a good rhythm at each gait – but this can be
nurtured to produce a horse who puts real power and
flair into his work. The use of half-halts and the introduction
of lateral work help the horse to become more balanced
and bring him nearer to working in self-carriage.

THE HALF-HALT

The half-halt describes what happens when the rider closes his or her legs and hands momentarily against the horse. This serves to rebalance the horse at whatever gait he is working; the rider's legs push the horse's hind legs underneath him further while the hand blocks any acceleration in pace that the horse might offer. The power that the legs have created is trapped by the rider's hand so that instead of accelerating, the horse lowers his hindquarters and elevates his forehand slightly, becoming better balanced and lighter in the rider's hand. The half-halt can be used to (1) rebalance

HALF-HALT AT TROT

1 This horse is producing an active trot, and is maintaining a good outline; considering that he is young the overall picture is soft and round. The rider is sitting quietly with the leg aid on, but only needs to maintain a light contact with the reins to the horse's mouth.

2 Now the horse is becoming unbalanced. He has probably overpowered himself with the push from his hind legs and is poking his nose forward and starting to lean on the bit in an attempt to balance himself. The soft, round outline is disappearing.

3 To rebalance the horse, the rider uses a half-halt. She closes her legs on the horse's sides and pushes him up into her hand which, just for a second, is blocked against the horse's forward movement. In effect, the horse's body is squashed up together; his outline becomes shorter because his hind legs are pushed further under his body so he is able to carry more weight on them, which in turn lightens and elevates his forehand.

4 The horse is rewarded by the rider relaxing the leg and softening the hand again. The softening, or giving of the rein, has been exaggerated in this picture to show that once the horse is using his hindquarters and hocks more actively he is able to carry himself and remain light in the rider's hand (self-carriage). So although the rein is completely loose, the horse is maintaining his own balance and a correct outline.

HALF-HALT AT CANTER

1 Here you can see how this horse is falling on to his forehand at the canter. The impression in the picture is that the horse's weight is falling forward and that he is leaning on the bit and, therefore, on the rider's hands for support.

2 The rider uses a half-halt to rebalance – she closes her legs against the horse's sides and blocks any forward acceleration with her hands.

3 Now the horse is balanced and light in the rider's hands. In picture one the hindquarters appear higher than the shoulders (on the forehand). Now the shoulders are higher than the hindquarters (the forehand is elevated and lightened).

the horse at any gait, (2) warn the horse that the rider is about to ask him to do something such as change direction and (3) build impulsion within each gait that can be stored to produce collected work, or released to produce extended work.

■ ACHIEVING THE HALF-HALT

Every horse will respond to a combination of hand and leg. You have to find out what combination is needed for your horse to obtain the desired result. Too much hand and the horse will either resist by throwing his head up, or he will simply slow down. Too much leg and the horse will try to accelerate and be pushed on to his forehand, which will unbalance him.

First, practise the half-halt at the walk. At a given point, close your legs against the horse's sides and reduce the degree to which you allow your hands to follow the contact, as if you were about to halt. Just as you sense the horse is about to halt, soften

THE RIDER'S SEAT AS AN AID

The rider's body weight can be used, through the seat, to influence the horse – it can create or block the amount of impulsion that the horse is working with. If you think about using your seat as an aid too soon, there is a risk that you will simply become stiff in your body and will no longer be able to move with the horse. The use of the seat will develop naturally once you have achieved that all-important independent seat. If you think back to the use of the hands and arms, and how these stay soft and relaxed so that they follow the movement of the horse's head and neck, that is how you should think of your own body weight. Just as you can change

the degree to which your hands follow the head and neck movement, when asking the horse to slow down or halt, for example, your body weight can be used either to encourage the horse to use himself more actively, or to slow him down. Letting the seat move freely with the horse encourages active movement; reducing the degree to which the seat moves with the horse slows him down. The use of the body weight or seat should always be subtle and sympathetic. The feel for its correct use will come naturally once an independent seat has been achieved, and once you understand how and why you need to influence the horse.

your hands forward again, keeping your legs on the horse's sides so that he continues at the walk. Once you get the feel of how much leg and hand is needed to produce this effect of almost but not quite halting the horse, you will have achieved a half-halt. Then practise it at the trot and at

the canter. Each time, act as if to bring the horse back to the slower pace and, at the last second, allow him to continue at the original pace. Once you have mastered the half-halt, you can use it more subtly to forewarn the horse that he is about to be asked to do something different.

TOO MUCH HAND

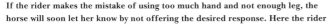

If the rider makes the mistake of using too much hand and not enough leg, the horse will soon let her know by not offering the desired response. Here the rider has tried to rebalance the canter by raising and pulling back with the hands, with no back-up from the leg. The horse responds by simply falling back into the trot.

DEVELOPING LATERAL WORK

The shoulder-in and half-pass are the most useful lateral-work exercises in terms of encouraging the horse to use his hocks more actively and effectively underneath him. The mistake that many people make is to think of them simply as requirements of a dressage test. This is not how they should be viewed – lateral work is used to improve the horse's overall way of going. These exercises teach the horse to respond to different uses of the hand and leg, to be supple through his body, and to place his hocks further underneath him in an effort to carry more of his body weight on the hindquarters rather than on the forehand.

COMMON FAULT

A common mistake is for the rider to ask for too much angle so that the horse works on four tracks instead of three, i.e. each leg is put down in a separate track. The rider has crossed her inside hand over the horse's withers so that the horse is only bending from in front of the withers, through the neck, instead of through the body and neck. The whole point of the exercise has been lost; the horse is not supple through the body, only through the neck, and the hind legs are not being encouraged to take any extra weight at all. To correct this mistake the rider needs to take up more contact in the outside hand to reduce the bend in the neck, use the outside leg to keep the quarters from swinging around any further, and the inside leg to push the shoulders back toward the track, which will reduce the angle of the horse's body until he is working correctly on three tracks.

■ SHOULDER-IN

The shoulder-in is similar to haunches-in, in that the horse moves on three tracks, but here it is the shoulders that are brought in, not the quarters, as the horse continues to move forward. The footfalls are as follows: the inside track is made by the inside foreleg, the middle track by the outside foreleg and inside hind leg together, and the outside track is made by the outside hind leg.

It is quite difficult in a shoulder-in for the rider to keep the horse moving forward in a straight line. The horse may try to swing his quarters out one way, or may drift sideways instead of holding the position and moving forward in a straight line. If you are working in an arena it helps to do the following: As you bring the

SHOULDER-IN

1 It is easiest to practise lateral movement in an arena so that you have a straight edge to work along; here the rider is about to ride a shoulder-in at the trot down the long side of the arena. She has already ridden a 33 foot (10 m) circle at the trot in the corner that she is just coming from. This circle gives the rider an idea of the correct amount of bend that the horse should hold throughout the shoulder-in. To start the shoulder-in she goes to ride another 33 foot (10 m) circle, but, as soon as the horse's front legs have left the track to start the circle, she uses the outside hand to prevent him from continuing on the circle, and the inside leg to keep him moving forward along the side of the arena.

2 As the horse progresses down the long side of the arena in a shoulder-in, you can clearly see how he is working on three tracks (inside fore, outside fore/inside hind, outside hind). This exercise encourages the horse to be supple as he has to maintain a bend through his body and neck; it also introduces the horse to the idea of carrying more weight on the inside hind leg. As the inside hind leg touches the ground, you can see that it is placed directly under the horse's belly and beneath the rider. So at this point the horse is carrying much of his body weight, as well as the weight of the rider, on that inside hind leg.

3 To help keep the horse moving forward in a straight line while in a shoulder-in, the rider should look straight ahead and think of her outside hip as pointing the way forward.

HALF-PASS

1 To ride the half-pass, shown here at a walk, the rider would turn down the long side of the arena and ask the horse for a shoulder-in. Instead of continuing in a shoulder-in, he would then use the outside leg back behind the girth to push the horse's hindquarters across until they are almost directly in line with the shoulders. The outside leg stays in place telling the horse to move sideways, while the inside leg also keeps him moving forward. The outside hand controls the degree of bend through the horse's body and neck while the inside hand remains open, inviting the horse to step forward and sideways.

2 In a half-pass the horse must remain bent around the rider's inside leg so that he is bent in the direction in which he is moving. In this picture, the rider's outside leg can clearly be seen in use behind the girth to push the horse sideways. Half-pass can be ridden at the walk, trot and canter.

3 This picture shows how, in a half-pass, it is the outside hind leg that has to come across and under the horse, thereby having to take the weight of both his own body and the rider's. The exercise also encourages the horse to be supple through his body and, in particular, through his shoulders.

horse's shoulders in off the track, make sure you are looking ahead yourself and think of your outside hip as a pointer; if you imagine keeping your hip moving forward in a straight line, the horse's outside shoulder will move forward on the same line. The correct position for the rider in a shoulder-in is for the hips to stay parallel with the horse's shoulders, but for the shoulders to be held straight as if you are riding forward in a straight line as usual. You should look straight ahead.

■ **HALF-PASS**

In half-pass the horse moves diagonally across the arena, taking good-sized steps forward and sideways, and keeping his body bent in the direction in which he is moving. His shoulders are allowed to be just fractionally ahead of his hindquarters as he makes this movement. His outside hind and foreleg cross over in front of his inside hind and foreleg.

COMMON FAULT

As you try more complex movements be sure to maintain the correct basics. In the right-hand picture the horse has dropped behind the contact and is overbent. Whilst moving into the half pass the rider must keep the horse pushed up into the contact so that he continues to carry himself correctly.

VARIATIONS WITHIN EACH GAIT

The horse is capable of a number of variations in each gait, e.g. in trot or canter the horse can work at a collected, working, medium or extended gait. At walk he can work in a collected, medium, extended or free walk. As the horse's responsiveness to his rider increases and his training progresses, he should be able to offer all of these variations smoothly and without resistance. When asking the horse for variations within each gait, think in terms of asking for more power and impulsion rather than more speed.

MEDIUM WALK

The medium walk is the pace the horse naturally offers his rider – the sort of gait that would be produced out on a hack. The horse takes long, relaxed steps and he overtracks, which means his hind feet step further forward than the hoofprints left by the front feet.

▌ RIGHT
The medium gaits require the horse to work with increased impulsion so that he takes longer, rounder steps than he would do at the working gaits. He lengthens his whole frame slightly while still keeping a round outline.

WORKING TROT

The working trot is the gait the horse naturally offers his rider. It is an active gait with the horse maintaining a round outline while working in a forward-thinking rhythm. It is the sort of trot the horse would produce out hacking – relaxed but active. The same is true of the working canter.

COLLECTED TROT

At the collected gaits, which can be either walk, trot or canter, the horse shortens his whole outline by lowering his hindquarters and bringing his hocks further under him, and by elevating his forehand so that his neck is raised and arched. The horse takes shorter, rounder steps, with greater elevation.

MEDIUM TROT

EXTENDED TROT

At the extended gaits the horse stretches his whole frame and takes steps of maximum length with maximum impulsion. As with all the variations in pace, the horse must still remain in balance and in a rhythm. This horse could still afford to lengthen and stretch his neck a little more forward so that the overall picture is of a longer frame.

FREE WALK

◼ LEFT
The free walk is often asked for in a dressage test – the rider offers the horse a long length of rein and the horse stretches his head and neck down and takes long, relaxed steps forward, with his hind feet overtracking his front feet. Because the horse has been taught always to expect a contact between his mouth and the rider's hand, when the rider offers him a long length of rein, he stretches his head and neck down to seek out the contact he is used to feeling. To allow the horse to stretch his head and neck fully, the rider allows her arms and hands to go forward and down so that there is still a straight line from her elbow, through the arm, down the rein to the bit.

EXTENDED CANTER

At the extended canter the horse lengthens his whole frame and fully extends his legs to take the longest possible steps while still remaining in balance. Notice the really good elevation or 'lift' in his stride. This shows he has lengthened by really stepping under himself with his hindlegs and pushing forwards, rather than just flattening out.

ACHIEVING COLLECTION AND EXTENSION OF THE GAITS

Producing these variations within each gait involves bringing together the techniques and principles with which you should, by now, be familiar. Whether the horse is working at the collected, medium or extended paces, he has to maintain the same rhythm in his work. In other words, you do not slow the horse down in order to achieve collection, nor should you go faster in order to extend the horse. To achieve collection, the rider uses the half-halt so that the horse's hocks are pushed further underneath him while the hand prevents him from accelerating. The trapping by the rider's hand of the power produced by the use of the leg causes the horse to shorten his frame and put that power into taking shorter, higher steps. Medium or extended work is achieved by first using half-halts to collect the horse and then releasing that power and energy in varying degrees by softening the hand forward, which enables the horse to lengthen his frame and his stride. Whether the resulting gait is medium or extended depends on the degree to which the rider softens with the hand while continuing to ask for more power and drive from the hindquarters. To be able to produce these variations in pace, you have to develop a feel for creating and storing energy for collected work, and for directing that energy forward into either medium or extended work.

COLLECTING AND EXTENDING THE HORSE

1 When practising collecting and extending the horse, it is easier to work within the confines of an arena. The short side of the arena which provides two corners in close proximity to each other is a good place to ask for collection, while the long side, or even across the diagonal, provides room for extending the gaits. This rider is using half-halts to collect the horse as he progresses through the corner of the arena and begins to turn down the long side. A corner is a good place to start to ask for collection, as the horse has to bring his inside hind leg further underneath him in order to negotiate the turn anyway. Notice the raised arched neck and the way the shoulders and neck are elevated because the inside hind leg is stepping further under the horse.

2 As he progresses down the long side the rider asks the horse to use the power of his hindquarters to lengthen not just the stride but the frame of the horse. By keeping the leg on so that the power continues to be produced the rider then allows the horse's neck and whole frame to lengthen by allowing forwards with his hand. The horse is still elevated through his shoulders but not to the same degree that he is in the first picture because he is now taking his shoulders forwards to create the longer stride.

3 As the horse and rider approach the corner at the end of the long side of the arena, they use this situation to shorten the horse's stride and frame. The rider keeps the leg on but instead of allowing forwards to the same degree with his hands that he did to produce the long stride, he keeps his elbows back closer to his body so that the hand is not allowing forwards so much. This shortens the horse's entire frame as well as his stride, as he is being squeezed up from the rider's legs into a hand that contains him.

INTRODUCING THE COUNTER CANTER

Counter canter is a movement required in many dressage tests, and it demonstrates the horse's suppleness, balance and obedience. Counter canter involves the horse cantering with the left leg leading while being worked on the right rein, and vice versa. The horse must keep his head and neck bent over his leading foreleg, so that he is in fact bent in the opposite direction to that in which he is moving.

Counter canter is introduced by cantering on the left rein across the diagonal to the opposite track. As the horse reaches the other side and turns on to the right

COMMON FAULTS

In this picture, the horse is still cantering with the right leg leading but, instead of maintaining the bend of his head and neck to the right, he has bent to the left, i.e. he is now bent in the direction in which he is travelling. The rider must correct this by opening the right hand and closing the right leg on the girth to ask the horse to maintain the bend to the right.

Another common mistake is for the horse to bend his neck too much to the right. This causes him to lose his balance and his whole body drifts back to the track instead of following the path of the 16½ foot (5 m) loop. When this happens the horse's hind legs are not following in the same tracks as the front legs – the horse is simply falling sideways or falling out through the shoulder. If the rider now took up more contact on the outside (left) rein to straighten out the bend of the head and neck, used the left leg behind the girth to stop the quarters swinging out to the left, and opened the right hand while keeping the right leg on the girth to encourage the horse to bend his neck to the right, the correct counter canter would be restored.

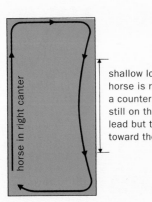

shallow loop where horse is ridden at a counter canter – still on the right lead but travelling toward the left

rein, he should be asked to maintain the canter with the left leg leading for a few strides, before being brought back to trot.

Once horse and rider are comfortable with this, shallow loops can be ridden at the canter down the long side of the arena; while the horse is on the track he is cantering as usual, whereas while he is negotiating the shallow loop he is in fact in a counter canter, provided he maintains the original bend of his head and neck over the leading foreleg.

RIDING A 16½ FOOT (5 M) LOOP IN COUNTER CANTER

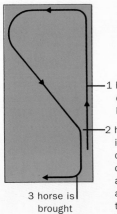

1 horse canters on left rein with left leg leading

2 here the horse is asked to continue in canter left although he is about to turn to the right

3 horse is brought back to trot

1 The horse canters around the arena on the right rein with the right leg leading as usual. Instead of continuing down the long side of the arena, the rider turns the horse off the track and rides a smooth 16½ foot (5 m) loop along the long side. As the horse negotiates the first curve of the loop he must continue to canter on the right lead.

2 As the horse negotiates the loop, he must maintain a very slight bend to the right throughout his body, so that he is correctly balanced in right canter, even though he will be travelling on a curving left line.

3 As the horse follows the loop around to the left and back towards the track, he must still maintain right canter. The rider will need to give good support with her inside leg and outside rein to prevent the horse dropping his weight on to his shoulders.

RIDING A FLYING CHANGE

The flying change is when the horse changes directly from cantering with the left leg leading to cantering with the right leg leading, and vice versa. It is called for in some dressage tests and can be built upon in more advanced dressage so that the horse can literally change from one leg to the other on every stride, almost as if he were skipping! For the average rider, the flying change is most useful when jumping a course that requires changes of direction at the canter. For example, instead of landing over a jump with the left leg leading, then having to come back to a trot before picking up a canter on the right lead in order to turn right to the next fence, the rider can simply land, take

a few strides forward at the canter and then ask for a flying change as he turns toward the next jump.

Before the horse can be asked to perform a flying change, he must be responsive and obedient to the leg, and his canter must be balanced and show a degree of collection. He should willingly perform walk-to-canter transitions, be able to produce 33 foot (10 m) circles at the canter, and work at a counter canter before progressing to a flying change.

Some horses tend to become excitable or nervous when they are introduced to this movement, so be sure to teach it carefully and patiently.

CHANGING THE LEAD

1 This movement is best taught by asking the horse to change from counter canter back to normal canter. This horse has been down the long side of the arena on the right rein, and has then cantered a half-circle so that he is now cantering across the diagonal with the right leg leading.

2 As the horse nears the track and the ensuing left-hand corner, the rider must indicate to the horse that he must change from right canter lead to left canter lead. The rider momentarily blocks the horse's forward momentum by closing and setting the left hand, while at the same time changing her leg aids from asking for the right lead to asking for a left lead, i.e. the rider's left leg is now applied at the girth, and the right leg used behind the girth to tell the horse to put his right hind leg down on the ground first. Remember that if the right hind starts the stride off, it is the left foreleg that appears to be leading. In this picture, you can see how the rider's left hand has blocked the horse's forward momentum so his forehand is elevated as a result.

3 In this picture, the horse is in the period of suspension that follows each canter stride, and it is only at this point that he is able to perform the flying change. So the blocking of the forward movement makes the period of suspension just a fraction longer, giving the horse time to rearrange his legs so that he lands on the opposite lead, i.e. he changes from the right lead to the left lead. This young horse has overreacted to the rider changing the position of her leg aids (bringing her left leg back to the girth and using her right leg behind the girth). He has flicked up his back end higher than his forehand which unbalances him. As he strengthens up and becomes more relaxed about the exercise he will make a smoother flying change.

4 As a result of the rider changing her aids from asking for canter right to asking for canter left, the horse has landed on the left lead as required and can now continue to canter around the arena on the left rein.

RIDING A DRESSAGE TEST

Once you have practised everything that has been discussed in this book so far, it will be good for both you and your horse to go out and put it all to the test by riding in some dressage competitions. These can be anything from small, local affairs to affiliated competitions.

Always make the effort to learn your dressage test by heart, but do not practise it continually on your own horse because he will learn it himself and will start to anticipate the next movement instead of waiting for your instructions. At some competitions you are allowed to have your test read aloud, but if you are having to concentrate on instructions being read aloud, you cannot possibly concentrate 100 per cent on getting the best out of your horse.

Your horse should be well groomed and have his mane plaited (braided) for a dressage competition. You should wear a pair of white or beige jodhpurs or breeches, long or short riding boots, a riding jacket and a shirt and tie or stock.

All dressage tests begin with the horse and rider coming down the centre line of the arena, and all but preliminary tests require the rider to halt the horse and salute the judge. This first movement is the first impression that the judge will have of you – the only thing the judge can see from that angle is how straight your horse is as he comes down the centre line. So concentrate on riding the horse forward in a good active pace, as it is easier to ride a straight line if the horse is moving forward with impulsion. (Think of how a bicycle wobbles if you pedal too slowly – the same happens to a horse if he lacks impulsion.) A good straight halt will earn you good marks and put the judge in a good frame of mind for the rest of your test. Be ready with both hands and legs to correct any attempt the horse may make to drift one way or the other as you squeeze him forward from your legs into a blocking hand and into the halt.

▌ RIGHT
Notice how this young rider is looking across the arena to the marker where she has to make her next move. Keeping your head up and looking ahead to where you have to go next helps improve the accuracy and timing of the different movements you have to perform.

Once the horse halts, keep a feel against his sides with your legs and down the rein with your hand. This will keep him on the aids and attentive to your next instruction. A smart, sharp salute will all add to the good impression. The correct way to salute is to put both reins in your left hand (while still maintaining a contact!) and to drop your right hand down to your side, bowing your head at the same time. In more advanced tests, where there is more than one judge positioned around the arena, it is necessary to salute each judge in turn. It is worth practising the halt and salute at home so that your horse is not surprised by the movement. When you are

Every single dressage test includes at least one – and usually two – halts and salutes. A nice straight halt and a confident, unhurried salute create a good impression, and are aspects of the test that can be practised at home.

ready to ride on again, concentrate first and foremost on straightness and maintaining a constant rhythm.

The various movements in a dressage test have to be carried out at the markers that are set around the arena. The correct point at which to carry out the next movement is as your shoulder is level with the marker. Always look up and think ahead to the next marker. Insist that the horse stays out on the track and uses the whole arena; do not be tempted to cut corners. If you ride the horse correctly around each corner, you will automatically be rebalancing him and asking him to use his hind legs more actively. Remember to balance the horse during and before each new movement, with a half-halt if necessary. All tests end with another turn down the centre line and a halt and salute for the judge. No matter how well or badly the test may have gone, always perform this movement with good grace and manners. Remember that each movement in the test is marked separately, so that if you make a mistake in one movement all is not lost. If you keep your cool and improve upon the mistake in the remaining movements, you will pick up marks again. Never give up – there are always more good marks to be earned. On top of all that, do make a conscious effort to smile. It will immediately fill you and the judge with confidence and, more importantly, it will help you to relax and to stay that way.

PREPARING FOR TAKE-OFF

One of the best things about riding is to experience the exhilaration of riding a horse over fences. A lot of new riders are put off by jumping due to a lack of confidence but, if you have developed any sort of feel for riding, jumping should simply be a natural and enjoyable progression.

All too often, when faced with a fence to jump, horse and rider seem to forget the basics they have been practising up until then. Balance and rhythm are abandoned as they career toward the obstacle! The secret of safe, enjoyable and successful jumping is to carry into the jumping arena the principles learned and mastered while riding on the flat.

RHYTHM AND BALANCE

The two most important things for the would-be show jumper to keep in mind are rhythm and balance. If you can concentrate on keeping the horse balanced and in an even rhythm all the way to the fence, you have very little else to worry about.

You have already discovered how to encourage the horse to work in an even rhythm and to be responsive to your leg. Just because a jump appears in your path does not mean that anything changes – the horse must still be obedient enough to stay in the rhythm that you have dictated and, provided that you learn how to stay in balance with the horse throughout, clearing the fence comfortably and confidently will come naturally to both of you.

Horse and rider can practise working in a balanced rhythm by simply trotting and cantering over poles on the ground. This kind of work can be mixed in with your usual flatwork training so that the horse learns to remain calm and to apply

WORKING OVER TROT POLES

1 The horse is ridden in an active working trot through the corner and down to a line of trot poles set approximately 4 feet (1.25 m) apart, which gives the horse room to put his feet down between each pole as he takes each stride.

2 The horse must stay balanced and in the same rhythm as he approaches the line of trot poles.

3 The rider softens his hands forward so that the horse is able to stretch his head and neck forward as he negotiates the poles.

4 The horse should maintain exactly the same rhythm throughout the whole exercise – do not allow him to slow down at the end of the poles. Ride him through the next corner correctly, insisting he bends around your inside leg and maintains his balance and rhythm, and repeat the exercise.

WORKING THROUGH CANTER POLES

1 Exactly the same exercise should be practised at a canter, except now the poles are spaced approximately 10 feet (3 m) apart to give the horse room to canter over them.

2 The rider must keep the horse balanced and in the same rhythm through the corner and all the way up to the poles.

3 As the horse negotiates the poles, the rider simply softens the hands forward so that the horse's head and neck are not restricted.

4 As when working over trot poles, the horse should maintain the same rhythm throughout the whole exercise.

5 As the horse completes the poles and canters on to the next corner, exactly the same rhythm and balance must be maintained throughout.

the same rules learned on the flat to his jumping work. Far too many horses are allowed, and often encouraged, to become overexcited and go too fast when they are asked to jump. The horse should be taught to use power to clear fences, not speed.

USING POLES AND LINES OF FENCES

Trot and canter poles are often used to help introduce horse and rider to jumping. They should be spaced out in such a way that the horse can easily negotiate them, without having to stretch himself or shorten himself up. Trot poles are usually set about 4 feet (1.25 m) apart and canter poles 10 feet (3 m) apart. But if these distances do not suit your horse, then, at this stage in his training, alter them to suit him. Adding lines of fences to the poles forms what is called a jumping grid. Gridwork is used to introduce the horse to the idea of jumping. Later in his training, it is used to increase his athleticism and to improve the way in which he jumps. It trains him to jump more carefully so he is less likely to injure himself or to knock fences down.

■ INSIST ON CONSISTENCY

It is only with practice and patience that you will teach the horse to carry out this exercise. Most horses thoroughly enjoy the idea of jumping but it is important to teach the horse to contain his enthusiasm so that he still remains obedient, balanced and in a rhythm.

A young horse who is being introduced to this work for the first time should have no reason to rush or get excited, provided he has been taught the basic principles throughout his flatwork training.

An older horse who already knows about jumping may get excited if he has been allowed to do so by previous riders, but practice and perseverance will teach him to keep an even rhythm.

If the horse really is inclined to rush, you should keep circling around the outside of the poles until he settles into a steady rhythm. If he still rushes as soon as he is allowed to go to the poles, simply circle him away from them again and keep repeating this exercise until he maintains the same rhythm. Alternatively, you can bring the horse back to a walk and insist

that he walks over the poles until he is prepared to keep the same rhythm at both a trot and a canter.

The opposite problem may occur with an inexperienced or nervous horse who may want to slow down on the approach to the poles until he is confident about what they are. The first few times the horse is introduced to the exercise, he should be allowed to slow down to give him time to take everything in. After that, insist that he maintains the same rhythm. It may be worth choosing a slow rhythm at the trot so that the horse does not feel he is being hassled, but do insist that the horse sticks to this rhythm throughout. Once he is confident, the pace can be picked up a little and a faster rhythm maintained throughout. The horse should never be rushed through these exercises – his pace should be active and yet balanced.

In jumping it is the power of the horse that is critical, not his speed. As a rider you are trying to create and store power and energy on the way to the fence so that all that power can be used by the horse to clear the fence.

JUMPING FENCES

It is your job to bring the horse to the fence in a balanced rhythm, to remain in balance with him over it, and to land in balance so that you can continue to the next fence.

Most riders attempt to do far too much on the approach and over a fence, which only unbalances and distracts the horse. When jumping at a canter, keep a light seat on the approach to the fence. About 22–33 yards (20–30 m) away, while still retaining exactly the same rhythm, lower your seat deeper into the saddle and actively close your legs against the horse's sides. Keep your shoulders slightly forward. Having closed the legs more against the horse's sides, you may have to take a slightly stronger contact in the hand to prevent the horse accelerating. As the horse takes off over the fence, remain in the same position but close your lower legs tighter against the horse's sides sides to keep you securely in the saddle, and allow your hands and arms to follow the forward movement of the horse's head and neck as he stretches over the fence.

BASIC TECHNIQUE

1 Here the rider is in the forward seat. Note how her seat bones are raised just off the saddle so there is less weight directly on the horse's back. This encourages the horse to remain soft through his back and to move along actively beneath her. The rider keeps her shoulders slightly more forward than they would be when cantering on the flat, but it is this position that allows the weight to be taken off the saddle while still allowing the rider to keep her balance. The lower leg is closed on the horse's sides, and the rider's weight is now taken by the stirrup iron. The horse is producing a light, active canter with his forehand nicely elevated.

2 As the rider approaches a fence, she lowers her seat into the saddle but keeps her shoulders in the forward position. The lower legs are closed more firmly against the horse's sides so that his hocks are pushed under him, but the rider's hands prevent him from accelerating. The aim is to collect the horse so that he has plenty of energy to power himself over the fence.

3 Just before the horse takes off, the rider softens her hands forward so he can lower his head and neck to produce a supple, clean jump. The rider's seat is still deep in the saddle, her lower legs are closed against the horse's sides, and her heels are pushed down. It may help to think of 'squatting down' just as the horse is about to take off, as this will avoid the temptation to lift your seat out of the saddle.

4 As the horse takes off, all the rider does is to allow her hands and arms to stretch forward to follow the movement of the horse's head and neck. The rider remains perfectly still and balanced over the horse and, in this way, leaves the horse free to jump athletically and comfortably over the fence.

5 By adopting this technique over a fence, the rider is able to remain in balance with the horse; this means that, as they land, the two of them are still balanced and ready to face whatever comes next. If another fence were to follow immediately, they would both be in the correct position to tackle it.

6 Horse and rider look equally balanced on the approach and on landing over the fence. If horse and rider can maintain this same rhythm and balance around a whole course, they have every chance of producing a clear round, be it cross-country or in a show-jumping arena.

COMMON JUMPING FAULTS

GETTING IN FRONT OF THE MOVEMENT

These two pictures show one of the most common faults of which any number of riders, of all levels, are guilty. Faced with a fence, many riders seem to be overwhelmed by an irresistible desire to anticipate when the horse is going to take off and to 'jump' with him! Instead of sitting quietly and maintaining their position, the rhythm and the balance, they fire their seat out of the saddle, hurl their upper body up the horse's neck and generally do about ten times more than they need to. The effect on the horse is both unbalancing and distracting.

This can result in the horse hitting the fence with his front legs because the rider has loaded too much weight on to his forehand or, worse still, the horse may be tempted to put his feet back down again in front of the fence. The horse is then unable to jump at all.

You can see how easy it would be for the horse to put his front feet back down on the ground and, because the rider has come right out of the saddle and thrown all her weight forward, she would have very little chance of staying on board. In the second picture, the rider is still in a relatively weak position; her weight is balanced on her knees instead of being pushed down into the stirrups and her heels, with the result that her lower leg has slid backward.

The rider is going to be out of balance with the horse as he lands and will not be in a very strong position to regain the balance and rhythm that they started with. If the horse stumbles as he lands, because the rider is not supporting her weight in her lower legs and heels, she will probably be thrown forward. Again she could fall off or, at the very least, she would not be able to help the horse recover as well as if she had maintained her balance.

IN TIMES OF TROUBLE!

While the horse must not be allowed to rush toward his fences, it is just as important that he is not allowed to slow down to the point that he runs out of impulsion and stops. If you sense that the horse is reluctant to keep progressing forward to a fence, you must adopt a more aggressive style of riding to encourage the horse to keep going. In this situation it is more important than ever that you keep your seat in the saddle the whole time. If you are tempted to anticipate the take-off and get in front of the movement, the reluctant jumper is presented with the ideal opportunity to stop dead!

In these pictures, the rider has pressed both legs very firmly against the horse's sides. If necessary, both heels should be used to kick the horse forward. The seat remains deep in the saddle and the rider arches her back slightly to allow her seat as well as the legs to drive the horse forward. The rider must not throw her hands forward at the horse as often happens – she is trying to ride the horse up into the contact so that while contact is maintained it does not actually restrict the horse's forward movement.

CHASING THE HORSE INTO THE FENCE

Another fault commonly adopted by any number of riders is to chase or rush the horse into the fence. The rider is meant to maintain the same rhythm and balance as he or she rides from fence to fence, but many people feel unable to wait for the fence. As soon as they are a few strides from it, they drive the horse forward, immediately unbalancing the horse and pushing him on to his forehand.

This approach usually results in the horse taking off much too far away from the fence and really having to stretch to clear it. In these pictures, even the horse looks angry at this unwanted interference from his rider. If the horse is made to jump like this, he is likely to knock fences down. He is being made to use speed to clear the fences rather than power and the athleticism of his body. If he is ridden like this cross-country, particularly to a very upright fence, he will find it difficult to get his front legs up in the air quickly enough and risks hitting the fence; if it is a solid cross-country fence, this would be enough to unseat his rider or, at worst, would cause the horse to fall as well.

■ RIGHT, TOP TO BOTTOM
In the first picture the horse's canter stride is already plenty long enough, but in the second you can see that the rider has continued to drive the horse, stretching out his frame and stride even further. Compare the look of this canter to the approach made in the first pictures in this chapter. In those pictures the canter looked light and active, and the forehand was elevated. In these pictures you can see how flat and stretched out the canter is and how all the weight is falling on the forehand.

MAINTAINING BALANCE AND POSITION

The easiest way to learn to maintain the correct position while jumping is to learn how to stay in balance with the horse – and the easiest way to learn that is to remember always to maintain the same rhythm when jumping. Having already practised maintaining the rhythm, balance and your position over trot and canter poles, this exercise can be extended to include your first jump about 14 feet (4.25 m) away from the last pole. You should simply concentrate on keeping the horse trotting in a balanced, even rhythm through the trot poles and on to the fence. The horse will fit in three trot strides after the last pole and will be perfectly placed to jump the fence.

If you find that you cannot resist the temptation to 'jump' as the horse jumps, or if you feel yourself tensing up as the fence gets nearer, try the same exercise without looking at the fence at all. It's quite simple, and the horse will cope perfectly well without your eyes looking out for him, provided you do still maintain the same even rhythm.

POSITION AT TAKE-OFF

1 Think about maintaining the correct position, keeping your seat in the saddle as you approach the trot poles but allowing the shoulders to be carried forward a little.

2 Close the lower legs against the horse's sides just in front of the fence, and soften the hands forward.

3 As the horse takes off, allow the hands and arms to go forward in order to follow the movement of his head and neck.

LOOKING AWAY FROM THE FENCE

1 Once you have lined the horse up in front of the row of ground poles, look to one side so that you cannot anticipate the fence itself.

2 Keep the rhythm throughout, sit deep in the saddle, allow your shoulders to move forward a little, and close your legs against the horse as he trots over the last pole (you will feel him do this).

3 As you feel him take off, just allow your hands and arms to follow forward.

TROTTING AND CANTERING TO A FENCE

Having experienced your first jump, it is now just a matter of getting the feel of cantering to a fence while maintaining the same principles as described already. This is most easily done by extending your existing line of trot poles and small fence to include a second fence, which the horse will jump from a canter. This should be placed approximately 18–20 feet (5.5–6 m) from the first fence; this allows the horse to trot to the first fence, land and take one canter stride before taking off over the second fence.

Many riders at this stage feel tempted to interfere in an effort to help the horse, but the grid is set up to allow the horse to find his own way through. The biggest help you can be to your horse is to maintain the even rhythm and balance.

JUMPING TWO FENCES

1 The horse trots over the ground poles and up to the first fence, just as he did in the previous exercise. The rider retains the same position and rhythm throughout.

2 Having allowed forward movement with the hands and arms over the fence, the rider now makes sure his legs are closed against the horse's sides to encourage him to canter forward in the same rhythm. As the horse lands, the rider's hands return to the normal position.

3 Here the horse takes the one canter stride that brings him up to the second fence; the rider continues to concentrate solely on keeping his position and the same rhythm.

4 The horse clears the fence, but the rider has anticipated the jump and has allowed his lower leg to slide back a fraction and brought his seat out of the saddle. The next time he comes to this fence it would be good practice for the rider to look away so that he cannot anticipate what is going to happen!

MAINTAINING BALANCE

■ RIGHT
This is another horse and rider completing the same exercise. In the second picture you can see why it is so important for the rider always to soften the hands forward on the last stride in front of the fence – see how this horse has really stretched his head and neck forward toward the jump before taking off. This is to be encouraged as it helps the horse to produce a powerful, athletic and round jump.

In the last two pictures you can see how this rider has kept her seat in the saddle, which has allowed her to land in balance with the horse and ready for the next challenge.

THE CIRCLE EXERCISE – BALANCE, RHYTHM AND TRUST

Trotting poles and grids make it easier for the horse and rider to keep their rhythm and balance – the real test is whether or not they can maintain the same principles when cantering to a single fence. One of the best ways to ensure this is to practise this very simple exercise. Build a small jump somewhere that allows you room to canter in a large circle to it, say on a 33 yard (30 m) circle. Pick up a canter and just practise maintaining a good, even rhythm as you canter around the circle, bypassing the jump to begin with. When you feel settled enough to jump, make sure that you stick to the same rhythm – don't speed up or slow down just because you are thinking of jumping. As you come on to the last quarter of the circle before the jump, sit deep into the saddle, close your legs against the horse's sides and contain him in the same rhythm with your hand, and then look away from the jump. Maintain the rhythm and allow the horse to look after the jump. As you feel him take off, allow your hands and arms to go forward to follow the contact. Have a friend standing in the middle of the circle to remind you not to look at the jump.

Practise jumping at different speeds on the circle – the faster you go the further away from the fence the horse will take off, the slower you go the closer he will

FINDING THE RIGHT RHYTHM

1 On the last quarter of the circle the rider sits deep in the saddle, closes the legs and hands to collect the horse while still maintaining the same rhythm, and then looks away from the fence.

2 The rider continues to look away from the fence, concentrating only on keeping the same rhythm and balance. Note how the horse, left undistracted by his rider, is totally focused on the fence.

3 The horse has the fence measured up and is about to take off.

4 The rider allows his arms and hands to follow forward while the horse clears the fence.

get before take-off, provided you maintain the same rhythm. This exercise will help you find the rhythm from which your horse jumps best. Once you get the idea

of trusting the horse and waiting for the fence, you can go back to looking where you are going, but return to this exercise whenever you get the urge to interfere.

LEARNING TO TRUST THE HORSE

1 Nine times out of ten, if the rider looks at the fence at this stage he or she feels obliged to interfere by either checking or chasing the horse. This simply distracts and unbalances the horse.

2 The rider is trusting her horse to do the job; note how the horse is fully concentrating on the task in hand and is about to clear the fence.

3 A horse can jump as big a fence as you wish in this way. Provided you keep the rhythm and balance, he will do the jumping.

IMPROVING HORSE AND RIDER'S JUMPING ABILITY

In the same way that, when learning to ride, the rider is more concerned about his or her own position and balance than about how well the horse is going, when learning to jump you must first master the art of keeping a balanced, rhythmic approach before worrying about trying to improve the horse's actual jumping ability.

Gridwork can be used to help in both instances – jumping the grids allows you to concentrate on improving your own balance and position, and can also be used to improve the horse's agility and ability over a fence.

Some horses are naturally more careful jumpers than others; some horses tend to throw long, flat jumps, while others may have a tendency to jump very high but with little scope to clear spreads. In either case, gridwork exercises can enhance the horse's performance.

■ **GRIDWORK AND JUMPING DISTANCES**

When gridwork is first introduced, the distances should be set to suit the horse. Once the horse is confident with the exercise, the distances can be altered – either lengthened or shortened – to improve the horse's technique. So with a horse who tends to throw a long, flat jump

the distance should gradually be reduced so that he has to collect himself up and use himself more athletically, while a horse who is very short strided should be encouraged to stretch out a little by using longer distances.

You may well wonder why it is necessary to alter what the horse does naturally. The reason is that, in the competition world, show jumps and cross-country fences are built to set measurements and distances. The course designer has to build fences that can be jumped safely by different sizes and types of horse, so he has to find an average distance to use and build his fences around that. For example, an average measurement used in course designing is based on the assumption that the horse will cover 12 feet (3.65 m) with every canter stride. Extra room has to be allowed for the distance away from the fence that the horse will take off, and further distance must be allowed on the other side of the fence for the horse to land. A rule of thumb is 12 feet (3.65 m) for one canter stride, plus 6 feet (1.9 m) for take-off and 6 feet (1.9 m) for landing. If the course designer wants the horse to fit in one stride between two fences, he will place the fences 24 feet (7.35 m) apart. To fit in two strides the fences

GRIDWORK DISTANCES

As a general guide, the following distances can be used in grids:
A bounce distance (where the horse doesn't take a stride between two fences but lands and takes off again immediately)
  at a trot – 9–12 feet (2.75–3.65 m)
  at a canter – 12–13$^{1}/_{2}$ feet (3.65–4 m)
One-stride distance approached
  at a trot – 18 feet (5.5 m)
One-stride distance approached
  at a canter – 18–24 feet (5.5–7.25 m)

would be placed 36 feet (11 m) apart – two canter strides equal two times 12 feet (3.65 m), plus 6 feet (1.9 m) for landing over the first fence and 6 feet (1.9 m) for taking off at the second fence.

If your particular horse is to fit in the same number of strides as the course designer intended, he needs to cover the ground that the designer has based his figures on. Higher up the competition ladder, the course designer may include an extra-long or an extra-short distance to test riders' ability to adjust the distance their horses cover. Some riders may choose to collect their horses and fit in three strides; others may push for two.

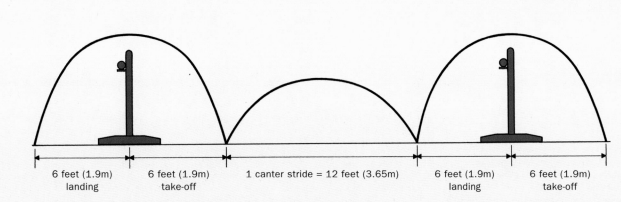

Jumping distances (left to right)

6 feet (1.9m) landing   6 feet (1.9m) take-off   1 canter stride = 12 feet (3.65m)   6 feet (1.9m) landing   6 feet (1.9m) take-off

BOUNCE GRID

GRIDWORK EXERCISES

Jumping grids can be adapted and altered as much as your imagination allows, the only confines being that you use distances that are acceptable and safe for the horse. But you should always have some aim in mind when designing a grid, otherwise you may dishearten the horse or simply end up undoing with one exercise any improvement you had created with another. So don't just go blindly on – feel the difference the grid is making to the horse and change it accordingly. And if the horse throws a truly fantastic jump early on in the session, it sometimes pays to stop at that point rather than risk undoing the good work you have just created.

It is very helpful to have someone knowledgeable watching you from the ground. Sometimes they can see, better than you can feel, exactly what the horse is doing as he progresses through the grid.

▌ RIGHT, TOP TO BOTTOM
The fences in this bounce grid have been set at 10 foot (3 m) intervals. The horse is introduced to the exercise by first using one bounce, i.e. two fences. This horse has approached this exercise at a canter, but if the horse has never seen a bounce before you may prefer to shorten the distance and approach at a trot, so that the horse has more time to work out what to do. When he is confident about tackling this, an additional fence can be added to make it a double bounce.

As you can see, a bounce distance means that the horse lands over one fence and immediately takes off over the next without taking a stride in between. It is a good exercise for improving the horse's physical and mental agility. He has to think quickly in order to organize himself correctly. Another advantage of this exercise is that it helps to make the horse confident enough to tackle lines of fences in competition. If he is used to seeing – and picking his way through – lines of poles and fences in front of him at home, he will feel more confident when faced with a complicated combination of fences in a competition.

Practising with a bounce grid also improves the rider's balance and ability to follow the movement of the horse.

■ THE COMBINATION GRID

This grid aims to improve the way the horse jumps. It starts with the horse trotting to a small cross-rail, set one canter stride away from a spread or parallel fence (oxer). This is set at a distance that suits the horse's natural stride. The distance to the parallel is increased gradually, by up to 2 feet (0.5 m), and the fence is altered to become an ascending parallel, i.e. the back pole is raised higher than the front pole. Once the horse is jumping well through this, it is altered again. This time the distance is shortened gradually, up to 2 feet (0.5 m) less than the original distance, and the fence is adjusted to make it a descending parallel, i.e. the back pole is now lower than the front pole. An ascending parallel encourages the horse to be neat and careful with his hind legs over a fence; the descending parallel teaches him to be neat and careful in front while still being able to stretch forward to clear the spread.

SQUARE PARALLEL

The horse is brought to the grid at a trot. The two trot poles are set 4 feet (1.25 m) apart and are, in turn, 8 feet (2.5 m) away from the small cross-rail (the first jump). These serve to bring the horse into the grid balanced and straight. He takes one canter stride before jumping the parallel.

ASCENDING PARALLEL

The approach through the trot poles and the cross-rail remains exactly the same. But the one-stride distance to the parallel (now ascending) has been increased. To encourage the horse to take a longer stride to help him cover the distance to the parallel, the rider simply 'clicks' to the horse and closes her legs against his sides to tell him to stretch forward. The horse responds by taking a longer stride than he did in the first grid sequence. In the last picture you can see how the horse is really using his hindquarters, and has snapped up his hind legs to make sure he clears the back pole.

RIDER'S WEIGHT

Here the horse tackles the same grid and, from this angle, the interesting point to note is shown in the last picture. The rider has, to some degree, thrown her body weight forward and up the horse's neck, rather than keeping her seat in the saddle. Note how she has thrown her weight to the left side and look at the effect this has had on the horse's left foreleg.

Because the rider's weight is over the horse's left shoulder, it is harder for the horse to bring his left foreleg up as quickly and cleanly as the right foreleg. It would therefore be very easy for the horse to knock this fence down with the trailing foreleg. To avoid this, the rider's weight must stay balanced centrally in the saddle.

DESCENDING PARALLEL

The approach to this exercise is the same as before, but the one-stride distance is shortened to less than it was in the very first grid, and the parallel is now descending. The horse has to land over the cross-rail, collect and shorten his stride and then be quick and neat with his front legs to clear the front pole of the descending parallel. The previous exercise will have reminded him to be really tidy with his hind legs, so this exercise should produce his most impressive jump. Note in the last picture how very neat and correct this horse has been with his front legs – exactly the aim of the exercise.

■ THE DOUBLE OF PARALLELS

This exercise is aimed at helping the horse who tends to jump high, but not necessarily very wide. Two parallel fences (oxers) are built one stride apart, with the distance set to suit the horse's stride, i.e. approximately 24 feet (7.35 m). The horse is cantered through this once or twice and then the distance between the two fences is shortened by simply making the two parallel fences wider – the back rail of the first fence and the front rail of the second fence are moved 1 foot (30 cm) or so toward each other. This encourages the horse to jump wider than usual over the first spread; he must land and shorten himself up to fit in one stride before having to make another scopey jump over the second spread.

INTRODUCING TWO PARALLELS

The exercise is introduced by cantering the horse to two parallels, set one stride apart at a distance to suit the horse's stride. Note how soft and sympathetic the rider's hands are – allowing the horse to use himself without restriction.

ADJUSTING TO THE JUMP

Now the spreads have been made wider so that the distance between the two fences has become shorter – the two green standards have been moved in toward each other. In the first picture you will see that the rider has been caught out by the huge jump that the horse has made – she really needed to allow her arms and hands to go forward more so as not to restrict the horse.

Having made such a big jump, the horse now has to shorten and balance himself quickly in order to clear the second fence. Note the improved position of the rider's hands.

RIDING RELATED DISTANCES

Over a whole course of fences, two of them will often be placed at what is called a related distance. This means the designer intends the competitors to ride a set number of strides between the two. Combination fences refer to jumps that are one or two strides apart, whereas related distances refer to jumps that are anything from three to, say, six strides apart.

Gridwork exercises at home will have shown you whether or not your horse has a naturally short or long stride, and you should use this knowledge to your advantage when faced with combinations

or related distances. If the horse has a naturally short stride, you will need to encourage the horse to open up his stride; you may need to ride with more pace than, say, the rider whose horse has a long, ground-covering stride. Whatever the case, when riding combinations or related distances the aim is to maintain an even stride length between the fences, not to land over the fence and then have either to check the horse or to chase him forward toward the next element.

Watch a number of horses tackling a related distance and you will start to see

how it rides best. Some riders may approach in a short, collected canter and fit in an extra stride, while others may let their horses jump, canter and jump out of a longer stride and fit in one stride less. If you practise the options at home you will learn which approach suits your horse, but whatever the number of strides you opt for they should be of an even length. So, to fit in the maximum number of strides, approach in a more collected canter, with a little less pace. To fit in the minimum number of strides, approach on a longer stride with more pace.

TAKING FIVE EVEN STRIDES

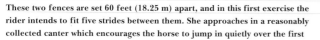

These two fences are set 60 feet (18.25 m) apart, and in this first exercise the rider intends to fit five strides between them. She approaches in a reasonably collected canter which encourages the horse to jump in quietly over the first fence. As she lands, the rider successfully maintains the same rhythm that she had on the approach, and this allows the horse to fit in the five even strides as required between the two fences.

TAKING FOUR EVEN STRIDES

Now the rider needs to open the horse up a little to fit in only four strides, so she approaches with a longer stride and in a stronger rhythm than previously. The horse jumps in more aggressively, which helps him to make up some of the distance required. The rider again thinks about keeping the horse going forward and in the rhythm that she had on the approach. This allows the horse to take four strides of even length between the fences. In the last picture you can clearly see that the rider has thrown her body weight far too far forwards. This is a common error, and thinking of 'squatting down' as the horse takes off will help you keep your shoulders up and your seat in the saddle.

TOO MUCH PACE

This rider, attempting the same exercise, shows how not to do it! Her plan was to fit in five strides, but instead of coming at a quieter rhythm than normal she has ridden the horse strongly into the fence so that he throws an extravagant jump. She is now going to struggle to fit in the five strides and resorts to checking the horse back, i.e. using her hands to make the horse continually shorten his stride. In the third picture, you can see how the horse is objecting to this treatment by throwing his head up and resisting the rider's hand. The horse has kindly cleared the fence for her but could easily have knocked it down, or even refused. Once the horse throws his head up, his eye is taken off the fence and he is unable to judge what he needs to do. It also makes him tense and hollow so that he cannot be as athletic. As you can see from these pictures, instead of taking five strides of even length, this horse's strides were being gradually shortened. Having made the initial mistake of coming in with too much pace, the rider may have been wiser to allow the horse to continue in the stronger rhythm and to fit in only four strides. Practising these exercises at home will give you a feel for how to get the distance right on the day and for how best to react when things go wrong.

RIDING A COURSE OF FENCES

Successfully riding a course of show jumps is simply an extension of the principles practised at home – except that you need to concentrate for longer. Instead of having to keep the rhythm and balance over just one or two fences, you have to maintain them around the twists and turns of a course. But the principle is exactly the same – choose your rhythm and stick to it. Keep the horse balanced, especially on the turns, and maintain that balance and rhythm every inch of the way around the show-jumping course.

■ RIDING YOUR ROUND

As soon as you have entered the arena, pick up the canter you will be jumping from and give the horse a good canter around and in between the fences. Always be aware of being in the right position to keep cantering around to the first fence once you start your course. You will be eliminated if you blatantly show your horse the fences before you

However large or small the course you are about to jump, always take the opportunity to walk it so that you can measure the distances between fences and decide the exact line that you intend to ride.

start, but if there is a particularly spooky fence in the arena it is a good idea to happen to canter past it on your way to the first fence!

Once you begin, stay relaxed and just concentrate on holding the rhythm and balance all the way around the route you have planned to ride.

Fences can come up on you very quickly once you are jumping in a competition arena, so look up and ahead the whole time. Look for the next fence before you have even landed over the previous one. If you have to land over a fence and then turn, say, right to the next fence, open your right hand slightly once you are in the air over the first fence, and just bring your left leg back behind the girth at the same time, to encourage the horse to land and canter away with the right leg leading. If you fail to get to the turn with the correct leg leading, either ask the horse for a flying change or bring

Make good use of the practice jump. Keep it very low to begin with so that you both get a confident and happy start to your warm-up. Then gradually raise it to the height of the fences in the ring. If things start to go wrong for any reason, put it back down and jump it a few times until you are both confident again.

WATCH THE COMPETITION

If there is time, try to watch several other horses and riders negotiate the course. In a jumper course, listen for the judges' signal to start – usually a bell, buzzer or horn – and remember that you must start within thirty seconds of hearing it.

Watch to see whether or not each of the distances between the fences is riding as you envisioned. Are the horses finding the distances long or short?

Note the turns that the other riders make to the fences and see which route appears to give the horse the best chance of clearing the jump.

■ RIGHT
The aim is to have a happy partnership, as is illustrated here.

WALKING THE COURSE

At some show-jumping competitions the rider is given the opportunity to walk around the course before the class starts. Make the most of this time to note the following relevant points:

■ Find the start markers. In a jumper course, you must pass through these once you get the signal to start, or you will be eliminated.

■ Walk the route you intend to ride. Do not simply take the shortest line from fence to fence in order to learn the order of the course. Walk exactly where you intend to ride and memorize it.

■ As you walk, note the conditions of the ground – are there any parched or slippery areas to try to avoid? Pace out the distances between any combination or related-distance fences. Remember that 24 feet (7.35 m) equals landing, one stride and take-off. Every stride after that takes 12 feet (3.65 m). So a one-stride distance between the fences is 24 feet (7.35 m), a two-stride distance is 36 feet (11 m) etc.

■ As you walk any turns, ensure that you really are allowing enough room to get the horse straight and lined up for the next fence. Do not be tempted to cut corners at this stage.

■ Relate the distance that you measure out to the knowledge you have of your own horse's stride length. You will know from practicing at home whether your horse covers the ground easily or whether you need to open him up in order to fit in the designated number of strides.

■ Note where the finish markers are. In a jumper course, you have to pass through these once you have jumped the last fence.

him back to a trot and then pick up the correct canter lead. If you simply let the horse canter on around the corner on the wrong lead he will be less balanced. There is also a risk that he will attempt to change on to the right lead but may only change his front legs, rather than the hind legs as well. This is called cantering disunited and is very unbalancing for horse and rider.

If you have to pass the entry/exit gate during your round, just be aware that your horse may be tempted to try to join his friends in the collecting ring. Keep your leg on and back it up with a tap from your stick if the horse drops back from the rhythm you asked for.

If you do have a refusal or a runout, make sure you go far enough away to give your horse a good approach on your second attempt. It is very easy to panic and just swing the horse around and fire him at the fence again, which will only invite a second refusal. Turn him away, pick up the canter and make a good, balanced turn back to the fence. Do not be tempted to go faster and chase the horse into the fence – that will only push him on to his forehand and make it easier for him to stop again. Think of collecting him and riding him from a strong, determined leg up into your hand. Contain the power you are creating and channel it toward the fence. Keep the rhythm consistent and do not get in front of the movement.

Make use of the turns to collect and balance the horse. Remember that to go around a corner properly he has to bring his inside hind leg further underneath himself, which in turn helps to lighten and elevate his forehand.

After jumping the last fence, bring your horse down to a trot and then a walk, reward him with a pat on the neck, and leave the arena at a walk.

If disaster strikes and you have a really bad round, remember that losing your temper is not going to improve things. Never punish the horse after his round – the time for a smack is the instant that the horse misbehaves. And never ever punish your horse with a yank at his mouth, or a jab with the spurs. If things have gone wrong, the place to put them right is back at home. Learn from what happened – analyze the mistakes and use exercises at home to correct them. Then come out another day and do it right!

Once you start jumping a course of fences, you will find that everything comes up on you very quickly. You must keep looking ahead to the next fence so that you can plan your turns accordingly.

CROSS-COUNTRY RIDING

Riding cross-country is a true test of a horse-and-rider partnership – whether it be the genuine article, when you are quite literally crossing the open countryside and jumping whatever natural hazards block your path, or the more organized version of riding a course of cross-country fences. Cross-country riding requires bravery and fitness from both horse and rider, as well as obedience and trust from the horse. Cross-country fences do not fall down. Very often the horse cannot even see where he is going to land, and he cannot judge the depth of any water which he might be required to jump into. Far from being a sport for the reckless, cross-country riding requires trust, obedience and technique.

CROSS-COUNTRY JUMPING

▌ BELOW
When galloping cross-country your weight should be kept out of the saddle, unless riding downhill or directly on the approach to a fence. This allows the horse to stretch out underneath you unhindered by your weight in the saddle.

Jumping cross-country fences involves exactly the same principles of rhythm and balance that have already been discussed. The two main differences are:

■ You are generally required to ride cross-country at a faster pace than you would ride a course of show jumps. It is harder to balance a horse when he is traveling fast, so the rider has to work harder to achieve the same balance as when show jumping while travelling in a faster rhythm.

■ The terrain and the types of fence that you have to jump are far more varied than when show jumping. The cross-country course designer will use the natural terrain of the countryside to add to the questions he is asking of horse and rider. He might place a fence right at the top of a hill, or on a hillside. He may set the course so that the rider has to cross some rougher, more uneven ground on the approach to a fence, making the job of balancing the horse harder still. If you are riding cross-country while out hunting, for example, you will have no idea of what kind of terrain or fences may come up next. Whatever the countryside throws at you, you have to find a way of crossing it.

SPEED CROSS-COUNTRY

When riding in a cross-country competition there is nearly always what is called an optimum time to aim for, laid down either by the appropriate rule book or by the event organizer. Anyone exceeding the optimum time will incur time penalties. This often results in riders trying to finish the course faster than they are capable of doing. It may be good to be competitive but it is always better for the horse, and for the rider's long-term success, for horse and rider to finish the course safely rather than fast. You should never ride faster than you can ride safely.

Remember that you will have a better round, and probably record a faster time, if you settle in a rhythm and jump from that rhythm, than if you set off too fast and then have to fight for control in front of every fence. So think long term – ride your horse safely so that he learns how to deal with things properly and, just as importantly, so that his enjoyment and confidence grow. Gradually you will find you are recording good times cross-country without realizing you are even trying. That is how you produce a good cross-country horse.

DOWNHILL APPROACH

▌ ABOVE As you approach an uphill fence you should elevate your shoulders so that you lighten the horse's forehand; this makes it easier for him to get his front end up in the air and clear of the fence.

On the downhill approach to this fence, the rider keeps his seat well back in the saddle, and uses his legs and hands to keep the horse together so that he does not fall on the forehand. Just in front of the fence the rider elevates his shoulders slightly to lighten the horse's forehand further and to make it easier for the horse to get his front end up and over the fence. The rider must land in balance with the horse, ready to restore the balance and rhythm immediately.

COPING WITH THE TERRAIN

Keeping the horse balanced and in a rhythm across all kinds of terrain is the secret of good cross-country riding. When galloping on the flat in between fences you should adopt a forward seat, i.e. raise your seat off the saddle so that your weight is carried down through your lower legs into your heels and the stirrup irons.

In the same way that you use a combination of legs and hands when riding on the flat to keep the horse balanced and in a rhythm, do the same cross-country. You must be physically fit and strong to do this, as you not only have to support your own weight by keeping your seat out of the saddle, but you must also continue to use your lower legs effectively to keep the horse pushed up into your hand so that he is balanced. In front of a jump, do the same as you would when show jumping – lower your seat into the saddle, close your leg and hand sufficiently to keep the horse together and to keep him in the same rhythm, and then let your hands follow the horse's movement over the fence.

When galloping uphill, shift your weight further forward so that the horse's hindquarters are free to propel him up the hill. Still adopt the forward seat, but bring your shoulders further forward to keep your weight forward. Although

■ LEFT
Just as when working on the flat or show jumping, the cross-country rider must keep the horse balanced between her legs and hands, over all kinds of terrain.

uphill fences can look imposing, the horse will generally jump them very well as he is already actively using his hocks. On the approach to an uphill fence, slightly elevate your own shoulders, and drop your seat down into the saddle. This has the effect of driving the horse's hocks up underneath him and lightening his forehand so that he is able to raise his front end easily to clear the fence.

Downhill fences are harder to negotiate. When running downhill the horse is more likely to fall on to his forehand, which unbalances him and usually results in him leaning on the rider's hands for support. With all his weight falling on to his forehand he may not be able to raise his shoulders and forelegs quickly and cleanly enough to clear the jump. A good number of cross-country falls occur at downhill fences simply because the rider has failed to follow the golden rule of maintaining

balance and rhythm. So when riding downhill, keep your seat in the saddle, your weight well down in your heels and your lower legs pushed slightly forward. There should be no need to lean back unless it is an exceptionally steep slope. Do not let the horse pull his head and neck down because in so doing he will pull you forward out of the saddle and then all your weight, as well as the horse's, will be on the forehand. Keep your shoulders up, use your legs and seat to drive the horse's hocks under him and use a stronger contact to balance the front end. Elevate your shoulders more in front of the fence to help the horse lighten and raise his front end, and give his head and neck plenty of freedom over the fence. As you land, keep your own weight back so that you don't get pushed on to the horse's shoulders. Take up contact, close the lower legs and work on rebalancing the horse and restoring the rhythm again.

PREPARING FOR THE UNEXPECTED

When competing at a cross-country event, the rider walks the course and is therefore familiar with the terrain and the questions that the fences ask. The horse, however, has no idea what is coming next, and it is your task to use your knowledge of the course to prepare the horse.

Having left the start box, settle the horse into a good strong canter. Any straightforward single fences are jumped out of this canter; you simply have to maintain the same rhythm and balance and allow the horse to jump out of his stride. But when you know a more complicated jump is coming up, you must prepare the horse for it. So if you know that after the next rail there is a ditch to be jumped just one stride from it, prepare the horse for this unexpected obstacle.

On the approach to the rail, slow the horse and collect him so that his stride is shorter but he is still in an active rhythm. Hold this strong, more collected canter all the way to the rail. An experienced horse will take this as a signal that there is more to this fence than meets the eye. It gives him time to realize that a ditch follows the rail. On an inexperienced horse, this same action will help focus the horse's attention on the fence, and will give him time to see the ditch on the other side. However, you must be prepared for the horse to be wary of the ditch, and you may need to ride more aggressively so that he keeps going and tackles both the rail and the ditch that follows.

Similarly if the next fence is followed by a step down, or involves a combination

of various obstacles, always re-collect and balance the horse on the approach. If, having walked the course, you know that the distance between two fences is very tight, shorten the horse's stride on the approach and keep this new rhythm all the way to the fence so that the horse jumps it tidily and has room to take the designated number of strides. If there is a long distance between the fences, open the horse's stride up well before he gets to the jump and hold the new rhythm all the way to the fence. On landing you may need to send the horse forward actively in order to encourage him to continue the opened-up stride on the approach to the second fence.

Landing over a drop or into water also requires some warning for the horse, and

JUMPING INTO WATER

On the approach to this log into water, the rider has shortened the horse's stride and really pushed him together. This has elevated the horse's forehand and has helped to focus him on what is coming up. Just in front of the log, the rider is ready with a strong leg to insist that the horse keeps going now that he has spotted the water on the landing side of the fence. The rider keeps her upper-body weight back as the horse drops down into the water, and she slips the reins through her fingers to allow the horse the full use of his head and neck. Once in the water there is not enough time for the rider to shorten the reins again; she therefore draws her elbows back behind her, which in effect takes up the slack in the reins and allows her to regain the contact and control.

you should rebalance and collect him on the approach. As the horse lands, use your own body weight to help balance him. Make sure you don't get tipped forward; keep your body weight back by keeping your own shoulders elevated. Although the reins will have slipped through your fingers so that the horse's head and neck are not restricted over the jump, you still need to keep a contact with his mouth so that you can help balance him again as

you land. If the horse trips or stumbles as he lands, or if he is taken by surprise at the size of a drop, or by landing in water, you can use the contact through the reins to support the horse and to keep his head up slightly, and you may well be able to save him from falling. In contrast, if you have leaned forward and let the reins go loose, if anything untoward should happen on landing both you and the horse are likely to fall.

■ ABOVE LEFT
When jumping into water, you must keep your weight well back. However, at the same time it is vital that you let the reins slip through your hands so that you do not restrict the horse's use of his head and neck. Note how this rider maintains a contact so that he can help to balance the horse as soon as they have landed in the water.

■ ABOVE RIGHT
When cantering through water the rider must keep a contact with the horse's mouth so that the horse can remain balanced and light on his forehand.

It is quite difficult to stay in balance with a horse when he jumps up on to a step or bank. The idea is to keep your seat close to the saddle, but with your weight just raised out of it so that the horse feels he can really use himself. Your upper body needs to fold forward and your hands must also move forward so that, once again, the horse has enough freedom of the rein to stretch and use himself as he jumps.

PATIENCE AND DETERMINATION

You can spend a lifetime mastering the art of horsemanship because, like any artist or craftsman, it is perfection that you are seeking. You may not wish to take your riding to the highest levels but you should never close your mind to the opportunity to improve. You may have no ambition to compete seriously but you should always have pride in the care and well-being of your horse. Enjoy him to whatever degree you wish but always repay him by making sure you know how to care for him. Every horse and pony, whatever his job in life, deserves to be looked after properly.

Those who do wish to strive for perfection will need patience and determination in equal measure. Patience is vital because all horses are individuals, and some will react and learn more quickly and easily than others. You must be prepared to take time to teach the horse the basics so that you have a strong foundation to build on later. A horseman should always be working for the long-term good of the horse, not for short-term gain.

Determination is needed because somehow horses always seem to create as much

heartbreak as happiness. Things do go wrong – some horses simply aren't cut out for the sport for which they were bought. In the same way that not all human beings can cope with the same pressures or stresses in life, horses vary in their degree of tolerance and aptitude. Many a failed competition horse has become someone else's adored hack or hunter. So always be realistic about what you are asking of the horse. If he really isn't up to the job, it is kinder to sell him to someone who will appreciate his other talents, rather than for both of you to endure a life of frustration and misery.

Horses do go lame or become ill, often just before your main target of the season, and riders have accidents with a similar degree of bad timing! Years of work and preparation can appear to be wasted when such things go wrong, but if you have trained and prepared your horse thoroughly and carefully your chance will come.

You will never stop learning about how to get the best from your horse. Even the top riders continue to go to people more experienced than themselves for help and advice – and remember that they never stop practising their art either.

COPING WITH AN EARLY TAKE-OFF

This rider has taken quite a risk at this widespread fence by asking her horse to take off very early. On a less scopey horse there is every chance that this sort of riding will result in a fall, as the horse may be physically unable to clear the spread of the fence and will land on it. In the first picture the rider has kept the horse balanced and in an even rhythm, but in the second picture she has suddenly opened the horse up and asked him to take off. Had she maintained the rhythm and balance all the way to the fence, the horse would have been able to fit in another stride and would have taken off a little closer to the fence. As it is, having taken off early, the rider has reacted in the correct way over the fence. She has kept her body weight balanced over the middle of the horse and has let the reins slip so that he can really stretch himself out and clear the fence.

TACKLING TWO CORNERS – 1

This horse and rider are tackling a combination of two corners set three strides apart. See how the rider lands over the first corner and, using his knowledge of his horse's stride length, he sits quietly and lets the horse take three even strides to the second corner.

TACKLING TWO CORNERS – 2

Another horse and rider tackling the same combination. Note how this rider, having landed over the first corner, knows that she has got to open up her horse's stride in order to make up the three strides to the next fence. She has sat down in the saddle and is really riding the horse forward. Knowing her horse very well, she has even dropped the rein contact with his mouth, and thus lessened her control, to encourage him to stretch everything forward in order to reach the fence. In this instance, it has paid off for her because she knows her horse well enough to trust him. Usually at a fence like this, which demands accuracy, you cannot afford to drop the rein contact in this way as the horse is then free to run out if he so wishes.

■ WHEN THINGS GO WRONG

Successful cross-country riding requires an ability to cope with the unexpected – even though you may have walked the course and know exactly how you intend to ride everything, sometimes the horse has other ideas. Despite your best intentions he may jump or react differently from how you imagined. Then you need to know what to do to make the best of the situation. For example, if your horse is normally long strided you might expect him to make up the distance in a combination easily, but if there is something in that combination that makes the horse back down, such as a ditch under the jump, suddenly you may not take off at the distance you imagined. Experience will teach you whether it is best to shorten your horse's stride and let him fit in an extra one, or whether you are better off riding even more aggressively, forcing him to open up his stride again and to take the fence. Some horses jump very big over ditches, or off drops, and this may alter the distance to the next fence.

Most importantly, if and when the unexpected happens, you are of most help if you can stay in balance with the horse and give him the necessary freedom of his head and neck. This all comes down to having an independent seat. If you can stay balanced without needing to hang on to the reins, and can at the same time keep thinking ahead and judging what you need to do to help the horse, you are the best asset he can have. A horse can jump out of some seemingly impossible situations, and can correct seemingly disastrous misjudgements, if his rider is not hindering him. The golden rule is to maintain rhythm and balance.

WORLD OF
THE HORSE

THE COMPETITION WORLD

Competing with your horse can be as low-key or as serious as you wish to make it. Some riders make a living out of riding and competing with horses, others simply enjoy giving the family horse a quick wash and brush-up once a year for a local show. Whatever you opt for within that scale, there are certain things to be aware of. Before attempting any form of horse sport you must be sure that your horse is fit and mature enough, both mentally and physically, to take part. He should be sufficiently well schooled to be obedient to your commands, and should have seen enough in his daily hacks and general training regime not to be overawed by the competition scene. Most horses should be versatile enough to take part in any number of sports at the lower levels. But if you decide to take up a particular sport seriously, check out the requirements and skills needed to ensure that you are both suited to that sport.

TYPES OF COMPETITION

▌ BELOW
There are so many opportunities to compete; all abilities and tastes are catered to, from the rough and tumble of mounted games...

The wide range of horse sports that is now available means there is something to suit all types of horse and rider. From the more genteel, such as showing and dressage, to the rough and tumble of team sports such as polo and horseball, all manner of skills, both mental and physical, are tested. Some sports are judged very subjectively. Dressage and showing, for example, are reliant on the opinion of the particular judge on the day. Others are out-and-out contests of stamina and tactics, such as horse racing and endurance riding. In show-jumping and cross-country riding competitions, the skills of each horse and rider are not only pitted against their fellow competitors, but also against the questions set by the course designer. However great or small your competitive streak, there is something to suit all tastes.

▌ LEFT
The main aim of competing at any level is that it should be fun. It is not so much the winning that is important – although everybody likes to win sometimes!

HEALTH REQUIREMENTS

■ Some affiliated competitions may state the age at which horses or ponies are allowed to compete in that particular discipline. For example, event horses are not allowed to compete in some events until they are five years old. You will need to be aware of such restrictions before planning a competition season with your horse.

■ Competition horses must have an up-to-date vaccination certificate that proves they have received their annual vaccination booster.

■ As a rider and competitor you have a responsibility to your horse and to other competitors to ensure that, if you suspect your horse is suffering from something contagious, he is kept isolated from other horses. Obviously if your horse is clinically ill you would not consider taking him to a competition but some diseases, such as ringworm or mild viruses, do not greatly affect the horse's general well-being. When this is the case you should not be tempted to hope for the best and still go – you must keep your horse at home, away from other horses, until he is fully recovered.

■ BELOW
...to the sheer
elegance of dressage...

■ RIGHT
...and the test of all-
around horsemanship,
eventing.

■ AFFILIATED AND UNAFFILIATED COMPETITIONS

Most countries have a good selection of organized horse sports, and these are usually split between what are regarded as affiliated and unaffiliated competitions. The **affiliated competitions** are generally stricter and require horse and rider to be registered as members of that particular sport's governing body.

At the top end of the scale, the International Equestrian Federation (FEI) governs all international competitions involving the sports under its jurisdiction – dressage, show jumping, carriage driving, eventing, vaulting and endurance riding.

The FEI controls their rules, and approves the programme of events at the regional, championship and Olympic level.

Each country's own national federation is, in turn, answerable to the FEI. They organize competitions for all levels of experience within their own country.

Unaffiliated competitions, usually run along the same lines as the affiliated competitions, are put on by individuals who are happy about taking on the organizational responsibility. To enter these you do not need to be a registered member of any governing body, but you will need to be familiar with the affiliated rules as these are often used. Many of

the riders who compete in the affiliated competitions will take advantage of the more relaxed atmosphere at unaffiliated shows to introduce a young horse to the sport. The unaffiliated competitions also act as an introduction to the sport for novice riders.

■ RESTRICTIONS

Many sports split their competitions into classes for either different age groups of riders, or different standards or sizes of horse or pony. Pony classes are restricted either to recognized pony breeds or to any equine standing under 15hh. Showing classes are classified by size and type of horse or pony – working hunter, show hack, cob, etc.

The affiliated organizations run competitions for horses of the various grades recognized by their governing body, e.g. event horses are graded from novice through to advanced, dressage horses from preliminary through to grand prix, and so on.

Local unaffiliated classes are divided up into rider age groups, size of horse or pony, or prize money or placings previously won. The novice class may be restricted to horses or ponies who have never been placed in any competitions,

the next class may be limited to horses who haven't previously won a competition. The open class, as its name suggests, is open to any grade of horse or pony and is usually the most competitive of all.

To avoid disappointment and embarrassment or, worse still, elimination, do make sure you have read the rules and regulations of any competition you intend on entering and comply with them.

The happy winner of a show class in England salutes his appreciative audience.

CHOOSING A SPORT

It is a good idea to find out if you enjoy and have an aptitude for a particular sport by entering unaffiliated competitions before going to the expense of registering with an affiliated body.

If, for example, you decide that dressage appeals to you, start out by competing quietly against friends and neighbors at local unaffiliated shows. Having decided that this sport really is for you, register with your national federation and start to work your way up through the grades of affiliated competition. If you have the talent, dedication and time to commit to the sport, there is nothing to stop you from reaching the top. If your sights really are set on the giddy heights of world championships or the Olympics, do remember that competitors at this level not only have to qualify to take part but also have to be selected by their national federation to enter as individuals or team members.

If you are lucky enough to be able to take your sport that seriously, you should investigate the opportunities that your national federation offers. Most countries that have an affiliation to the FEI also offer training to their members, as well as competitions culminating in international championships for riders of different age groups. The sports of dressage, show

▌ LEFT
When choosing a sport to take part in, it is important to consider the suitability of both your own and your horse's temperament. For some horses the excitement becomes too much – can you cope with this? Will it add to your fun or will it worry you?

▌ ABOVE AND BELOW
If you wish to compete regularly then some form of transportation is going to be necessary. This can be a vehicle and trailer or a horse box, either of which can be purchased, hired or shared. Not only will the trailer or truck provide a safe haven for your horse in between classes, it will also tend to become the social centre of the event.

EQUIPMENT NEEDED FOR ALL EQUESTRIAN SPORTS

■ You should wear a certified safety helmet or crash hat complete with safety harness for all horse-riding activities. If you intend to ride and jump cross-country, you should also wear a body protector.

■ Each sport has its own recognized and accepted style of dress. Dressage, show jumping and showing classes require the rider to be wearing a riding jacket, jodhpurs or breeches, short or tall riding boots and a hard hat. For cross-country riding, you can wear a sweat shirt instead of a riding jacket.

Polo, horseball and polocrosse require breeches and tall leather boots to be worn, along with a shirt instead of a riding jacket, plus protective padding such as knee pads.

Endurance riders wear either standard jodhpurs or breeches, or more lightweight ones for hot conditions, as well as rain gear for wet weather. They are not expected to wear riding jackets but dress according to the weather conditions.

■ Your horse or pony will need a well-fitting saddle and bridle, and it is also advisable to protect his legs against strains or scrapes by using boots or bandages.

■ You will need water, buckets, sponges, sweat scrapers and towels so that the horse can be washed and dried off if he is hot and sweaty after competing.

■ RIGHT
This competitor rewards her horse with a pat and a swim at the World Equestrian Games Endurance competition. Endurance competitors are allowed to dress according to the weather conditions.

jumping and eventing have championships specifically for pony riders, juniors and young riders. When you reach the age of twenty-one, you have to join the senior ranks.

Within the other equestrian sports there is usually a very good choice of competition designed to cover all levels of ability and ambition. In the showing world this ranges from local shows to regional competitions, right through to national championships. For some of these classes, your horse or pony may have to be registered with a breed society or showing association; these, in turn, help to govern and organize the various competitions, local and national.

Team sports such as polo, polocrosse and horseball require greater organization and facilities, as does learning the skills of vaulting. To take part usually entails joining a local club.

■ BELOW
Whether you have a good or a bad day, you must always put your horse's or pony's needs first. Make sure he has time to relax and enjoy the experience as well.

■ BELOW
Equestrian sports involving jumping offer variety and fun. Show jumping, for example, has classes available for anyone from leading-rein contenders, through junior classes as shown here, to international senior competitions.

TRAVELLING EQUIPMENT

Once you decide to compete regularly, unless you are very lucky in having regular competitions held within hacking distance, you will need to transport your horse in either a horse box or trailer. The horse must be kept safe and comfortable when travelling.

■ There should be bedding on the floor to cushion his legs and to help soak up any urine or manure he produces.

■ He should be secured with a headcollar (halter) and rope that is tied through a piece of string attached to the fixed tie ring. This is so that, should the horse fall or struggle, he will be able to free his head and neck – otherwise he may injure himself very badly.

■ He will need a selection of rugs (blankets), chosen according to the weather conditions on the day, so that he becomes neither too hot nor too cold on the journey.

■ He should wear protective boots or bandages on his legs, a tailguard or bandage (or both) to protect his tail from rubbing, and a poll guard to protect the top of his head.

■ You should offer your horse water to drink during the journey, and a haynet, although this should be taken away at least an hour before he is due to be ridden. Take food and hay for him to eat during the day and on the journey home, and keep a check on how warm or cold he is while travelling.

NON-JUMPING SPORTS

Horse sports are so varied that they are difficult to categorize. For the purposes of this book, they are split into a selection of non-jumping and jumping sports. To make it to the top of any one, you need to specialize. But most riders enjoy taking part in a number of different activities, so first look at the different things you can try. Unless you have your heart set on one particular sport, it is worth experimenting to find out what really suits you and your horse. The discipline and perfectionist nature of dressage may suit your personality, or perhaps you would prefer the more light-hearted approach of mounted games. Once you have outgrown those, there are team games such as horseball, polo and polocrosse to enjoy, or perhaps Western riding appeals to you. Whoever you are, whatever your ability, there is bound to be something to which you can aspire.

MOUNTED GAMES

▌ BELOW
Some games rely on your pony's skills; others are
down to the rider. In 'Apple Bobbing' you have to
retrieve an apple from a bucket of water without
using your hands!

If you can envision a cross between party games and a race on horseback, you will have some idea of what mounted games involve. Mounted Games are enjoyed by all ages of riders through the International Mounted Games Association, and through The Pony Club whose members are children. The beauty of these games is that there is one to suit every type and ability of pony and rider.

Mounted games can be organized for fun between a group of friends or as a serious form of competition, with regional, national and international championships provoking great rivalry between the various clubs and associations taking part. But at whatever level they are played, mounted games will help to develop your riding skills, your confidence in handling yourself and your pony and, most importantly, the realization that riding is fun.

■ HOW MOUNTED GAMES BEGAN

Surprisingly for a sport that is now dominated by children, mounted games were first played by adults. It was in India that the games we are familiar with today developed. They were then known as gymkhanas, which translated as gymnastic or athletic displays on horseback. The word *gymkhana* is still used in many countries today to describe the sport. The British Army, which was based in India in the late nineteenth century, adopted the games, although their mounts included donkeys, mules and camels. The games, such as 'Kiss the Girl', 'Tent Pegging' and 'Grab the Hat', were a popular and light-hearted way not only of helping to keep horse and rider fit and supple, but also of fostering strong regimental loyalty.

When the soldiers returned to Britain, they introduced the games to their home country where they proved most popular with children, their small, nimble ponies being ideal mounts for the games. The Pony Club, which was formed in 1929 and quickly grew to become a worldwide organization with over 100,000 members, developed and spread the benefits of the games. Pony Club Mounted Games are now played in over twenty-five different

countries at interbranch, interstate and international level.

For those who do not wish to lose out on the enjoyment of mounted games once they are over Pony Club age, there is the International Mounted Games Association. They hold World and European championships annually, in different host countries, for teams and individuals. Other opportunities to play mounted games are offered at local shows and gymkhanas, where there are classes for leading-rein competitors as well as for older children.

■ SKILLS REQUIRED

To enjoy mounted games for the fun and entertainment they offer requires no great skill on the part of horse or rider. But if you want to be the winner of many ribbons, or to make it on to a team and compete more seriously, certain skills are necessary.

Your pony will need to be fit, obedient, agile and unflappable – he will encounter all kinds of strange objects in the varied races offered. Most riders opt for a pony who for most other sports would be

A flying start is a big advantage, whatever race you are in. Practise at home by gradually asking your pony to
go straight into a canter from the walk, and then from a halt.

█ LEFT
Another great asset is the ability to vault on to a
moving pony. It is a bit easier than it looks – if you
time it properly the pony's forward motion helps
propel you through the air and up on to his back.

You must be able to control your pony
with only one hand on the reins, as the
other hand is often needed to do whatever
the game entails. If the pony can be taught
to neck rein, i.e. to respond to pressure on
the neck from the rein rather than to a feel
on the bit, controlling him with both reins
in one hand will be easy.

■ TRAINING YOUR PONY

Obedience in the form of quick responses
is what is required of the mounted-games
pony. He must be able to start and stop
quickly, turn tightly and, amidst all the
excitement of the race, remain stock still
while his rider carries out whatever task the
game requires.

You cannot begin to improve your
pony's responsiveness until he is working
obediently to the basic leg and hand aids.
Unless he is already at the stage where you
can quietly ask him to go forward at the
walk, trot and canter, to halt, to turn left or
right and to move to the side, i.e. leg yield,
he is not ready to be asked to do anything
beyond this. As in all things, establish the
basics first and it will be easy to teach your
pony any number of new skills.

THE RANGE OF GAMES

Each year more and more ingenious games
are developed to test the pony's and rider's
speed, agility, co-ordination, fitness and
sense of humour!

The easiest games are designed for
young riders whose ponies are being led –
musical mats, musical chairs and musical
statues. The children are led around on their
ponies until the music stops, when they
must leap off and pounce on a chair or mat.
One chair or mat is taken away each time so
that the rider who finds him- or herself
without a chair or mat is out. In musical
statues the pony, rider and leader must
remain absolutely still when the music
stops. The first to move is out – more often
than not it is the pony who doesn't have the
patience or desire to remain still.

For those who want to test their speed
and agility there are the races. These can be
as simple as a bending race, where horse
and rider thread their way between a line
of poles, or as complex and extravagant as
such team races as the 'Dragon Race'.
There are even games that include the fun
of jumping. In 'Chase Me Charlie', the
competitors follow each other over a jump.
If they clear it they stay in the game, if they
knock it down they are out. The jump is
raised each time until only the winner
remains. 'Barrel Elimination' involves
jumping over a line of barrels. After each
round, one barrel is removed so that the
jump becomes narrower and narrower until
there is only one barrel remaining to be
jumped over. If the pony stops or runs out
to either side, he is out of the game.

considered a touch too small for them,
but a smaller pony makes it easier to reach
down to deposit or retrieve objects and to
mount and dismount on the move.

As a mounted-games competitor, you
too will need to be fit and agile. Good
co-ordination and balance are called for,
as well as a good turn of speed as, in many
games, the rider may be dismounted and
leading the pony for much of the race.
Similarly, the ability to vault on to your
pony while he is cantering along is a
great asset, as is the ability to dismount
at speed without losing your balance
and falling.

█ LEFT
The Ball and
Racket race is
a game you
could easily
play at home.

■ LEFT
It helps to be fit and supple and to have good
co-ordination. Here the rider has to retrieve
a tennis ball from the top of the cone.

GETTING USED TO THE EQUIPMENT

In a serious mounted-games competition your pony will face any number of strange objects. He must be prepared to go up to whatever the target of the game is, he may have to go under a clothes-line strung with laundry, or a post hung with signboards – all kinds of items have to be acceptable to him. He must allow his rider to carry flags, buckets, swords and balloons without being worried by them. He must be accustomed to noise and the general hustle and bustle, including a very noisily appreciative audience, which is all part of a mounted-games competition.

All these strange and startling things should be introduced to the pony at home. As long as you give him time to realize that none of these peculiar objects is going to harm him, he will soon accept them. There is no point in using force – his trust has to be won and this takes time and patience. When you show your pony something new, allow him time to make up his own mind that it is harmless. Do not force him to approach a strange object too quickly. Reward and reassure him all the time that he is prepared to face it, even if he is still not very close to it. Only become stronger in your riding if he actually turns away from the object. Then you must be positive and use your legs and hands to turn him back. Once he is facing it again, reward him. Let him know you are displeased each time he tries to turn away, and gradually he will

realize that you are determined that he will meet this new thing.

■ RIGHT
Mounted games aren't just for children and small ponies – here an American Quarter Horse shows how good he is at bending. You can try this at home using a line of flexible electric fencing poles or barrels. Space them out at intervals and weave in and out of them keeping as tight to the poles as possible. Start in walk or trot then build up to canter.

■ BELOW
Mounted games are as much to do with teamwork as with individual ability and success.

THE GAMES

As you will have gathered, any number of mounted games can be dreamed up. The Pony Club probably has the most comprehensive list, which is used for their national and international competitions. It has a good rule book, including – to avoid any breakdown in international relations – an Official International Exchange Visits rule book. Despite the fact that mounted games are meant to be fun, they can become very competitive, so it is always safest to be sure everyone is agreed on the same rules. Here is a selection of some of the official Pony Club team games, but with a bit of imagination you can play a lot of these games at home with your friends and their ponies.

SACK RACE

Gallop your pony to the end of the arena where there is an empty sack. Jump off the pony, get inside the sack, and make your way back to the start, hopping, shuffling or tripping along, while still leading your pony. One trick is to rest an arm across the pony's withers as this will help support your weight and keep you upright. The other hand holds the sack up around you. Jump forward, allowing the pony to take your weight and to carry you forward a little way before landing again.

An even more amusing adaptation of this game is the 'Big Sack Race'. Four team members gallop to the end of the arena where a fifth team member is holding a huge sack. She takes her teammates' ponies while all four of them climb into the sack and, *en masse*, wriggle their way back to the start.

GROOM'S RACE

This calls for an additional skill – the ability to control two ponies at once. You have to ride your own pony, and lead one of your teammates' ponies, up through a line of bending poles. At the changeover point, your teammate mounts her own pony, and leads the third rider's pony back through the line of poles. And so it goes on until all the riders and ponies have had their turn and are back at the start.

LAUNDRY STAKES

One pair of riders gallops to a clothes-line, carrying a basket of laundry between them. They hang up the clothes and gallop back, handing the empty basket to the second two members of the team. They have to gallop to the clothes-line, remove the clothes, and bring them back safely to the start in the laundry basket.

DRAGON RACE

This is one of the most spectacular races to watch. It requires some quite elaborate equipment in the form of the dragon, and so it usually tends to be reserved for major championships.

The centrepiece is a model dragon with balloons attached to him. For added effect he is often made to puff great clouds of smoke. One team member plays the part of the damsel in distress, captured by the fearsome dragon. Her teammates are the knights attempting to rescue her. As a gallant knight, you race to the damsel and collect a token from her, which you tie to your lance. You then attack the dragon by bursting a balloon. When the last knight succeeds in bursting the final balloon, the damsel is rescued and led to the finish on her pony.

ROPE RACE

Set off at a gallop through a line of bending poles carrying a piece of rope about 3 feet (1 m) long. At the end of the arena, one of your teammates grabs the end of the rope and you both gallop back through the bending poles together. At the other end you drop your end of the rope and a third rider picks it up; the second and third rider hold the rope and gallop through the bending poles, and so on. Be careful not to allow your pony to step on the heels of the one in front.

▌ RIGHT
In the 'Dragon Race' the riders have to kill the dragon by bursting the balloons attached to him. Then they can rescue the damsel in distress.

■ RIGHT The greatest opportunities to play mounted games are provided by the Pony Club, which is an international youth organization.

IMPORTANT RULES

Most competitions are run under Pony Club rules. Points to note:

■ Ponies must be at least four years old, and not more than 14.2hh.

■ If you weigh more than 117 lb (53 kg) when dressed for riding, your pony must be over 12.2hh.

■ Your pony must wear a snaffle bridle and a conventional saddle; racing saddles are not allowed. Whips or spurs are not allowed, nor may you use the baton or your hand to encourage your pony to go faster.

■ Riders must wear recognized safety helmets with a proper safety harness.

■ The winner of the race is the pony who manages to get his head across the finish line first.

■ If the race involves leading the pony, the winner is the first rider across the line provided he or she still has hold of the pony. In a race involving pairs of ponies, the placing is judged from the moment that the second pony's head crosses the line.

BALLOON RACE

A bunch of balloons is tied to a post. Gallop to the post, collect a balloon, gallop back and pass it to your teammate. He or she gallops with it

■ RIGHT The greatest opportunities to play mounted games are provided by the Pony Club, which is an international youth organization.

to the post, collects a second balloon and hands both balloons to the third rider. This goes on until the last team member crosses the line with all the balloons in his or her hand.

STEPPING STONES

Race to a line of stepping stones – usually a line of upturned buckets or similar – dismount and negotiate the stepping stones while leading your pony alongside. Then remount your pony before crossing the finishing line.

BALL-AND-RACKET RACE

You have to balance a tennis ball on a tennis racket while riding your pony as fast as you can through a line of bending poles. You then hand the racket and ball to your teammate who races through the bending poles, and so on.

SHARPSHOOTERS' RACE

This race calls for another asset – a pony willing to carry two riders on his back! At the start of the race sit bareback on your pony. When the whistle sounds your teammate has to jump up behind you, and you race to the far end. Your passenger jumps off and has to throw soft balls at a row of comic figures until their heads are broken. Your passenger has to remount, and you both race for the line where the next pair of riders is ready to set off.

FISHING RACE

You are given a fishing rod, which is actually a piece of wood with a hook on the end. Gallop to a bin full of wooden fish with rings in their noses, hook a fish, gallop back to the start and hang it on a peg. Your teammate then sets off, catches a fish, brings it back, and so on until all the fish are caught.

■ LEFT
In the 'Stepping Stones Race', the rider has to tackle the stepping stones before vaulting on to the pony and racing for the finishing line.

PRACTISING AT HOME

There are plenty of games you can practise at home, either just for fun with your friends, or as practise for competitions. Use your imagination to adapt everyday household or yard items to use as props for your games but always keep safety in mind. Is the equipment likely to injure you or your horse, could you or the horse get tangled up in it? Use your common sense and you will have a lot of fun as well as learning many new skills. As we have already mentioned in the previous pages, both you and your pony need to be fit and supple to be successful. Teaching your pony to neck rein (see page 137) is essential as you will often only be able to use one hand on the reins, and taking time to introduce him to all the sights and sounds will help him to be confident and bold when taking part in the games.

EGG AND SPOON RACE

First you will need some spoons and some hard boiled eggs. You can play this game in one of two ways. Either you simply race each other over a set distance – if you drop your egg you have to dismount, pick it up and remount before you continue. Or if there are quite a few of you then you can make it a teams' relay race. Use some show jumping poles or something similar to mark a start and finish line.

Each rider can carry the egg and spoon over a distance before handing it over to the next team member who rides the same distance and passes it on to the next team member etc. Or each team member races with the egg and spoon to a bucket which they drop the egg in before racing back to the next team member who then does the same thing.

POTATO RACE

All you need is a bucket and a supply of potatoes! Again, this can either be a direct race against your opponent(s) or a relay style race.

■ ABOVE
Practising fun things such as mounted games will improve your partnership and confidence.

Use your imagination to invent and practise other games. You can take inspiration from the Pony Club Games but you don't need expensive equipment to have a lot of fun. Bales of wood shavings or hay can be spaced out and used for bending races. You can also use them for 'stepping-stones' races, for example. Race up to the line of bales, dismount, run along the line of 'stepping-stones' leading your pony beside you, remount and race to the line.

■ BELOW LEFT, CENTRE AND RIGHT
As you become more confident you can increase the pace you race at!

RIDING FOR THE DISABLED

The Olympics of 1952 marked the first year that women were allowed to compete alongside men in the Equestrian sports! If that was quite a shock for some people to take in, there was an even bigger surprise when a disabled rider, Lis Hartel, won a silver medal in the dressage competition.

Lis was born in Denmark in 1921 and became a successful dressage rider, competing at national and international level. But in 1944 she contracted polio and lost the use of her muscles from the knee down, as well as suffering problems with her hands and arms. Lis was determined to continue riding, and she proved to herself, and others, the therapeutic benefits of riding for those with disabilities. She followed up her success with another silver medal at the 1956 Olympics.

An inspiration to polio sufferers worldwide, Lis went on to found the world's first therapeutic riding centre, the Lis Hartel Foundation, which continues its work to this day. It did not take long for others to see the benefits of using horses as a therapy for people with both physical and mental disabilities.

▌ RIGHT
Riding for the Disabled Association (RDA) groups rely heavily on volunteers and donations. Parading at international events such as the Badminton Horse Trials helps to raise awareness and support.

A fellow rider, Elsebet Bodtker, who was also a physiotherapist, was inspired by Lis Hartel's example and started to provide pony rides to the young patients she was treating. Another, Stella Saywell, used the same ideas within her work as a physiotherapist at Winford Orthopaedic Hospital in England. The movement spread quickly within the UK in particular, with various generous and inspirational individuals offering riding opportunities to those with disabilities.

In 1964, the Advisory Council on Riding for the Disabled was formed, and this allowed the growing number of participants to exchange ideas and knowledge. As the movement grew and its great benefits were further realized, it was decided, in 1969, to regroup as the Riding for the Disabled Association (RDA).

Within the UK and Ireland, the RDA now offers riding, vaulting and carriage driving opportunities to over 25,000 disabled people. It is run almost entirely by its 18,000 volunteers. Whilst it is not officially an international organization, the RDA has offered advice and acted as an example for similar groups worldwide, with many countries now running their own similar groups. Most countries have a national championships where riders can compete in dressage, show jumping, vaulting and carriage driving.

A recent report published by the RDA showed that 80 per cent of RDA riders showed physical improvement in 12 weeks or less. The key therapeutic factor is the movement of the horse, which helps strengthen the riders' core muscles. A rider has to respond to the way the

▌ LEFT
Success, at any level, is down to a great partnership between horse, rider and support team.

▌ RIGHT
Sophie Christiansen, CBE, is one of the world's most successful Paralympic riders. She has won multiple medals – usually gold! – at the last 2008, 2012 and 2016 Olympic games, as well as numerous European and World Championship medals Sophie had to retire from the delayed 2020 Tokyo games due to a small veterinary issue with her horse, Innuendo III.

horse's body moves in walk, trot and canter, in order to stay in balance with the horse. The amount and range of movement that this requires is far greater than could be offered in a 'normal' physiotherapy session.

But added to that is the beneficial effect that horses seem to have on people's emotions and confidence. The instructors who teach disabled riders are trained to bring the best out of each individual. Some of the most severely disabled may always need assistance from the ground, and may never go faster than a walk, but the instructors are trained to use even this slowest movement to enhance the rider's physical and mental wellbeing.

At the other end of the scale are riders who go on to compete at the Paralympics. The majority of equestrian Paralympic competitors started their riding career through Riding for the Disabled Groups, and would have been coached and supported by these groups until they moved on to more specific and specialized training to achieve their Olympic ambitions.

■ EQUESTRIAN PARALYMPICS

Equestrianism became part of the Paralympics for the first time at the 1996 Atlanta Games. Athletes are graded into four different levels depending on the severity of their disability, which may be physical or visual. They can compete in individual and team dressage events, which includes a freestyle to music competition.

At the Atlanta Games there were 61 riders from 16 different countries, and all competed on borrowed horses. At the Athens Games in 2004, athletes were able to compete on their own horses for the first time. So inspirational has the equestrian Paralympics been that by the Tokyo Games of 2020, there were 200 athletes from 49 countries.

■ EQUINE-ASSISTED THERAPY

Using horses to improve the mental, emotional and physical well-being of people is a fast-growing therapy. It is particularly successful in improving people's confidence and communication skills, and has proved to be especially beneficial to those with post-traumatic stress disorder (PTSD) and autism.

Horses are very sensitive to human emotions and will often mirror the mental state of the person dealing with them. So if the person is calm and relaxed, so is the horse; if the person is fearful or angry, the horse will be tense and anxious.

There are many types of Equine-Assisted Therapy, but the basic premise is that a client is given certain tasks to perform with the horse, usually from the ground rather than as a riding therapy. The tasks may involve problem-solving, creative thinking, leadership or non-verbal communication. How the client tackles the task and how the horse responds provides an insight and potential to discuss the client's true emotions.

The simple fact that horses are large and powerful, and often intimidating to those not used to handling them, allows the client to quickly gain confidence and overcome fears as they successfully achieve the set goals, and this can be used to help them cope with other areas of their life.

THE HORSE BOY FOUNDATION

In 2004, a young boy called Rowan Isaacson was diagnosed with autism. He seemed completely unreachable, but his father, Rupert, found that his son was much calmer when he walked him in the woods around their home. On one occasion, Rowan ran off into a field of horses. To Rupert's amazement, the horses stood calmly around the crying, squirming child and lowered their heads to him, and he became completely calm. After that, father and son rode through the woods together everyday and, over time, Rowan began to talk and to engage with the environment and other people.

In 2007, Rowan and his parents travelled on horseback across Mongolia, visiting traditional healers to try to find a cure. They came home with a much happier, more engaging and communicative child. They set up the Horse Boy Foundation (a registered charity) with the aim of bringing Horse Boy therapy to all families with autism.

DRESSAGE

The simple aim of dressage is to produce a horse who can carry his rider easily, is supple, balanced, correctly muscled, active, eager and responsive to his rider's most subtle command – yet far too many people look down on dressage as an opt-out for those who are too scared to jump!

If you wish to succeed in any horse sport, you have a much greater chance of doing so if your horse is a well-schooled and responsive ride. Whatever sport or sports you decide to take part in with your horse, you should discipline yourself to practise the art of dressage, even if you never set foot or hoof in a competitive dressage arena.

Your horse cannot perform to the best of his ability, nor be a true pleasure for you to ride, unless he has had some help and training to improve his balance and responsiveness. A horse is a far greater joy to hunt, to jump, to hack out or to compete with in any form, if he is able to

balance himself so that he carries more of his weight, and that of his rider, on his hindquarters, which in turn will lighten his forehand.

■ THE HISTORY OF DRESSAGE

As far back as the fourth century BC, Xenophon, a Greek, wrote a book on training the riding horse. Prior to that, most interest in training lay in driving

▌ ABOVE
Practice makes perfect. This advanced combination is working on the dressage movement known as piaffe, which requires the horse to trot on the spot.

horses for chariots, rather than in riding.

From the sixteenth century onwards, a succession of European horsemen laid down the foundations of classical riding and training as we know it today. The aim of these early trainers was to improve the lightness and balance of the horse. Much of the work involved training from the ground using long reins, so that the horse learned the movements without the rider. Only after that was the rider taught how not to hinder the horse!

Interest in dressage fluctuated over the following centuries. In Great Britain there was far more interest in hunting and cross-country riding which, in those days, was performed very much on a wing and a prayer. The horses jumped what they were asked to jump either because they were naturally bold or because their riders were able to use enough brute force to get what they wanted. School riding or dressage was laughed at. Typically, instead of the good influencing the bad, in this particular instance the British attitude drifted across to France after the Napoleonic Wars, and the interest in dressage faltered there for a while. The nineteenth century saw a revival of interest in Europe. The principles laid down centuries before were refined and

▌ BELOW
Dressage arenas are either 40m x 20m or 60m x 20m (132ft x 66ft or 200ft x 66ft). The larger international size arena has additional letter markers to allow more complex movements to be carried out within the larger space provided. Even though there is more space to work in, the extra markers mean that new movements still come up very quickly. You have to think ahead and be as accurate as possible.

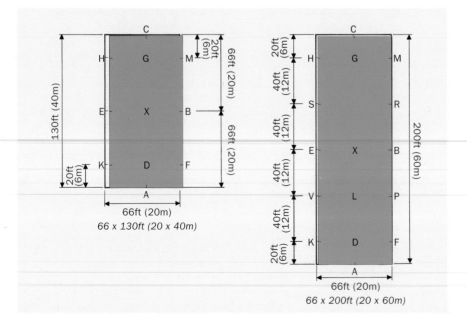

■ BOTTOM
Note how this rider is keeping a lovely soft contact while his horse remains in a nice outline and bent correctly in the direction in which they are going.

adapted, but the basic requirements of free forward movement, suppleness, obedience and lightness of the forehand remained and are still the aim of dressage riders today.

■ DRESSAGE AS A COMPETITIVE SPORT

Dressage is an Olympic sport, and its governing body is the FEI. It is therefore affiliated, and there are various levels of competition for affiliated members. However, dressage is a popular and easy sport to organize, which means that many unaffiliated competitions are run by various show organizers.

Dressage tests are split into the internationally recognized FEI tests and national tests, devised by each individual country. The national tests generally start with the lowest level, preliminary or novice, progressing through elementary to medium and advanced tests. Unaffiliated shows normally only offer classes up to elementary level, and may also make use of the simpler dressage tests taken from the sport of eventing. Most countries hold national and regional championships as well as participating in the international

FEI competitions. All tests are ridden in a dressage arena, which is a rectangle marked out by boards and letters. The letters signify where various movements should be carried out.

At the Olympic Games and other FEI championships, the arena must have an all-weather surface of sand, but at other competitions it may be of grass, or may be indoors.

Lower-level tests are judged by just one person, who awards marks for each set movement in the test, plus an overall mark for the horse's way of going and the rider's performance. The judge sits behind the C marker, in line with the centre line. Higher level competitions are judged by three or even five judges, who take up different positions around the arena. Their marks will vary as they see each movement from a different angle. The final score is an average of all the judge's marks.

■ ABOVE
The aim of dressage is simply to produce a fit, supple, obedient horse who is so responsive that his rider appears to be doing nothing.

In all dressage competitions, you are given a precise time at which your test will start. You must figure out how much loosening up and schooling work your horse needs so that he is well prepared for his test at the allotted time. Once you are sent over to the appropriate arena, you must not enter it until the judge signals you to start, usually with a bell or horn. You can ride around outside the arena, continuing to work on keeping your horse balanced, calm and attentive, until the judge's signal. Enter the arena at A and, if it is a requirement of your test, halt and salute at X. Most preliminary and novice tests only require a halt and salute at the end. To salute the judge, the rider is required to put both reins in the left hand, bow the head and drop their left

■ FAR LEFT
As the horse
progresses through
the levels, he is
expected to show
more expression in
his gaits. His outline
should be shorter
and higher, and his
gaits more powerful
and elevated.

■ LEFT
Great role models for
every rider – the smile
says it all. Charlotte
Dujardin and Valegro
complete another
inspirational Grand
Prix test.

hand to their side. After this, you can proceed down the centre line and into the first movement of the appropriate test. The test always ends with another trip down the centre line to halt and salute once more. Then proceed at a free walk, giving the horse a long rein, and leave the arena at A. After that, it is a case of waiting for your scores to be posted.

■ WHO CAN DO DRESSAGE?

Any rider can, and should, practise dressage, even if you choose not to compete. Once your horse is basically obedient, can maintain a rounded outline and can work in a reasonable rhythm at the walk, trot and canter, he is equipped

FEI TESTS

■ Prix St. George
■ Intermediare 1
■ Intermediare 2
■ Grand Prix
■ Grand Prix Special
■ Free Style Test – this is the same standard as the Grand Prix but is performed to music.

to perform the simpler dressage tests. The lower-level tests only require the horse to work at a medium walk, working trot and canter, and may require some lengthening of the horse's stride. The horse must be able to produce a good halt, as all tests end with a halt and salute to the judge, and the vast majority of tests also start with one.

International tests have to be ridden from memory, as does the dressage test in horse trials. In lower level tests you are allowed to have the test read out loud to you. But it is worth making the effort to memorize the test, both out of respect for the judge who has given up a day to come and mark you, and because to ride a really good test you need to concentrate fully on getting the best out of your horse, not wondering what command is going to be called out to you next. The movements of the test should become second nature to you if you are to ride your horse to the best of your ability.

■ SKILLS REQUIRED

To be successful in any equestrian sport you need to develop a secure independent seat but, in dressage, it is equally important

to develop 'feel'. You should be able to feel exactly what the horse is doing underneath you. Is he straight, is he giving you the correct bend, are his hocks really coming underneath him, is he relaxed enough through his neck and jaw? This feel can be developed with experience, but some riders are simply never able to accomplish it. Lunge lessons or lessons on an equine simulator are useful at any stage of your training to help you concentrate on your position and feel. Be patient and dedicated. The correct training of a dressage horse is a very long, careful process – there are no shortcuts.

It helps if the horse has a calm temperament and has good conformation and naturally good gaits. Ideally, he should be forward thinking with naturally active hocks, so he finds it easy to lower his hindquarters to carry out the more advanced movements. Finally, he should have presence – he should make people want to stop and watch him! But do not be deterred if you do not possess such a creature. Careful and consistent training can do wonders for the most unpromising candidate – it just takes more time and determination.

PRACTISING AT HOME

There are many ways you can practise dressage at home. In reality, the whole time you are riding you should be trying to embrace the principles of dressage. The aim of dressage is simply to enhance your horse's suppleness, athleticism, range of movement, the quality of his paces and his responsiveness to you as a rider. We should be trying to do this with every horse and pony. It makes him a safer, more enjoyable ride and, perhaps more importantly, it helps to reduce his injury risk as a supple, athletic body is less prone to injury.

■ ARENA MARKERS

You can practise whilst out hacking when the terrain and ground is suitable, but for more concentrated work it does help to have a marked out arena. The arena markers help you to be accurate and precise in your riding. For a 40m x 20m (132ft x 66ft) arena you will need 8 markers and, if you have space for a 60m x 20m (200ft x 66ft) arena, you will need 12 markers (see page 118). Make up your own markers using buckets or similar containers that you can fill with water or sand to keep

■ BELOW
With a bit of imagination it's easy to make your own dressage markers.

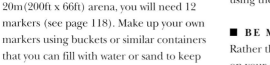

■ LEFT
Practise your test at home in front of friends and let them offer advice and ideas.

■ BELOW
If you enjoyed 'judging' your friend, volunteer to 'write' for a dressage judge at a show. It's a great way to learn.

them in position. Either paint the required letters directly on the container, or print them off on paper, laminate them and then fix them on. Put them in position using the measurements on page 118.

■ BE MY JUDGE

Rather than just practising a dressage test on your own, you can ask a friend to judge you. Use some old dressage test sheets and let your friend judge your test. Be kind to each other as, to be fair, you should take it in turns judging each other! If you take this seriously you can both learn a lot about what the real judge on the day will be looking for, and which parts of the test you need to practise more to earn better marks. The diagrams below illustrate some of the common test movements you can practise.

serpentine   half circles   16½ft (5m)

10m(3 3ft)

20m (65½ft)

THE WORLD OF SHOWING

The showing scene probably offers a wider range of opportunities for all types and abilities than any other equestrian sport. If you are the sort of person who takes pride in appearance, manners and performance – both yours and your horse's – you will enjoy exploring the showing world.

There are no Olympics or world championships for showing, but there is ample opportunity to compete. In most countries there are regional and national championships for the different categories of show horses and ponies.

If you wish to compete at the higher-level shows, you will need to register your horse with the appropriate society, usually a breed society, a show-pony society, or a hunter or hack society or association. Small, local shows do not usually require their entrants to be registered with anyone.

In terms of expense and facilities required, it is a relatively easy sport to accommodate. A grass enclosure and

■ LEFT
Traditional cobs and Mountain and Moorland ponies are shown in a more natural state. Their manes and tails are left unplaited (unbraided) and their legs are not trimmed either. There is a lot of work involved in keeping flowing manes, tails and feathers clean, shiny and untangled for these classes but, as this traditional cob demonstrates, the end result can be very impressive.

some respected judges are all that most classes require. Generally speaking, there are classes available to suit all ages and types of horse and rider.

■ IN-HAND SHOWING

Mares and foals, yearlings, and two-, three- and four-year-old horses and ponies can all be shown 'in-hand', i.e. they are led by their handlers and are judged on how well they are turned out, their conformation, their manners and paces, and their potential suitability for adult life. As the handler, you are expected to be very neatly dressed yourself, and your horse should be sensible and obedient enough to stand in line with the rest of the class, and to walk and trot in-hand when he is required to do so by the judge.

Your horse should appear in the ring

without a saddle, and with no boots or bandages of any sort. He can be led with either a halter or a bridle.

You can practise all the requirements at home, teaching your horse to halt squarely and to remain still, and to walk and trot calmly beside you when asked.

■ BREED CLASSES

Some classes are restricted to particular breeds so that the entrants can be judged on their trueness to type. Each breed of horse or pony should have certain

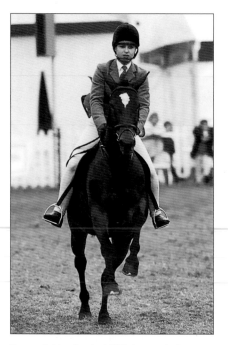

Pony and rider showing off their paces in the Working Hunter Pony class.

EQUIPMENT NEEDED

For nearly all showing classes, apart from side-saddle, you can use your normal saddle and a simple snaffle or double bridle, but if you want to specialise in showing you should invest in a saddle that is not too forward cut, so that you can show off your horse's shoulder rather than cover it up. Tweed or dark jacket and jodphurs or breeches and boots should be worn. Traditionally top hats, bowlers and velvet caps without chin straps were commonly worn for showing but as accidents can happen anywhere it is worth putting pride aside and wearing an approved hat with safety harness.

In many classes you have to be able to show off your horse at the gallop despite the confines of the arena. A safe, all-weather surface is provided for this show cob.

▌ RIGHT
To succeed at showing, you have to put great effort into the grooming and tidiness of yourself and your horse. This is an immaculately turned-out show pony and rider.

▌ BELOW
In some showing classes all the competitors ride around together while the judge assesses them. They are then asked to line up, after which they may be given individual tests.

NOTE: In the USA, the individual tests are usually only given in certain equitation classes such as Medal or MacClay, and could involve jumping.

SUCCESS IN THE SHOW RING

To maximize your chances of success in the show ring it is worth making use of a little ring craft. All this involves is using your common sense to ensure that the judge gets the best chance to view your horse. When you are all going around the ring together, make sure you keep some open space around your horse. If everyone is bunching up, circle away to make some more room for yourself. Do not hold your horse back and make him tense, as this will restrict his pace. Let him stay in his natural rhythm and circle away to make room.

If you are asked to give an individual test, remember that the aim is simply to demonstrate your horse's gaits, obedience and general way of going. Have something planned before you go in; do not do too much at the walk as this takes up so much time, and the judge will have had plenty of opportunity to view your horse at the walk already. Make sure you demonstrate the trot and canter on each rein. Keep your movements simple and smooth so that your horse is able to stay in a rhythm and in balance, and to show himself off to the best of his ability. Think of it as a short but sweet dressage test, using the same degree of accuracy and concentration in the show ring as you would in the dressage arena.

characteristics that identify him as being true to type. These characteristics are listed by the appropriate breed society. Breed classes can be judged either as in-hand or as ridden (under saddle) classes and, once again, turnout, manners and conformation are the key criteria.

Some breeds have very specific traits that they are judged on; for example, the Tennessee Walking Horse on his walk.

If the class is ridden, you are expected to wear jodhpurs or breeches with the appropriate short or tall boots, a shirt and tie or stock, and a hunting, show or hacking jacket. A helmet with a cover or a traditional velvet hat should be worn.

■ TYPE CLASSES

These classes are not restricted to breeds but to types of horse and pony. Within each type, the classes are often split by height or weight. The type of horse or pony might be working hunter, show hunter, show hack, cob, riding horse, three- or five-gaited horse, ladies' hunter, etc. The hunter and cob classes will probably be further divided into light-weight, middleweight and heavyweight, gaited horse classes may be divided by sex, while other classes are often split according to height or age of rider.

The classes designated 'working', such as the working hunter pony, involve the competitors completing a course of fences. These are usually rustic show jumps as opposed to solid cross-country fences, but may include a stile (coop), brush fences, a water ditch or a bank. It is usual for each competitor to jump their

▌ ABOVE
Many of the bigger shows are held indoors, with classes going on late into the evening. Your horse will have to become accustomed to spotlights and a far more claustrophobic atmosphere than he will have experienced at an outdoor show.

round, before the whole class is called into another arena where the judge will watch each one perform a short show designed to show off the horse's gaits, obedience and general presence. In very competitive classes, unless you jump a clear round you may not even be called back into the second arena for further judging.

In the other showing classes the usual procedure is for the whole class to walk, trot and canter together in a large arena watched by the judge. They are then all

■ LEFT
Equitation classes are popular, as riders are judged on how well their horses perform for them rather than on how epensive or well bred they look.

■ BOTTOM LEFT
Sometimes you will find yourself eligible for several different types of class. This young rider on her Welsh mountain pony can enter the leading-rein class as well as the Welsh mountain breed class.

■ BOTTOM RIGHT
Many classes are judged in-hand, which means that the horse is led rather than ridden.

■ SIDE-SADDLE CLASSES

Riding side-saddle used to be the only acceptable way for a woman to be seen on a horse but as horse sports became more popular with women riders, riding astride became the norm. However, such is the elegance and splendour of side saddle riding, that it is becoming ever more popular in many countries and side saddle classes are making a comeback. It is relatively expensive to take part because of the need for a side-saddle and riding habit – both items cost more than a standard saddle and riding outfit, but it is money well invested when you see the elegant result! There are many different types of Side Saddle showing classes and you may also ride side saddle in ordinary showing classes. In Side Saddle equitation classes it is the rider's ability and performance that is judged, not the horse's conformation or paces. This makes it a good class for anyone who's horse or pony wouldn't normally be considered the correct 'type' for showing. If you enjoy dressing up then Costume Concours d'Elegance classes may be just the thing for you as it involves wearing Period costume.

called into a line and all, or some, may be asked to perform an individual show in front of the judge. Additionally, the judge may want to ride your horse him- or herself, and to see him, untacked, walked and trotted up in-hand. A showing class may take a long time to judge and it is on these occasions that your horse's manners, patience, turnout and suitability to purpose will be put to the test.

PRACTISING AT HOME

Practise makes perfect and much of the success in the show ring comes down to immaculate turn out of horse and rider.

■ SIMPLE PLAITING

Perfect grooming, plaiting and quarter markers will all enhance the appearance of your horse or pony and, plaiting in particular, takes lots of practise if you want the best results. Divide the mane into equal bunches using rubber bands. With practise you will learn what size bunches produce the best plaits for your horse. You can also use needle and thread to sew the plaits in, but rubber bands are quick and easy for practising with.

■ RUNNING PLAIT

Mountain and moorland breeds, and cobs, can be shown unplaited, with full manes and tails. A full, free flowing mane and tail can look fantastic but for every day riding, that long mane can get in the way of your hands and reins. A quick and easy way to keep a long natural mane neat and tidy for everyday riding is to master the Andalucian or running plait.

1 Divide the first bunch into three equal sections and start to plait.

2 Keep the plait tight to the neck and equally tight all the way down.

3 Secure the plait with a rubber band. Then roll up or fold over the plait to create a neat ball.

4 Position the ball close to the neck and secure with a rubber band. Repeat along the mane.

1 Ensure the mane is well brushed through and free of tangles. Start with three bunches of hair and make an initial plait in the normal way.

2 Then keeping this first plait tight up to the crest of the neck, bring in another bunch of mane and introduce it into your next plait.

3 Continue like this, bringing in a new bunch of hair each time you complete a plait and keeping the whole thing tight up against the crest of the neck.

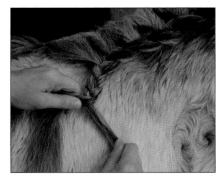

4 When you have plaited your way down to the wither, continue the plait as a pigtail and fasten with an elastic band.

5 Once you get the hang of this it is a very quick and easy way to plait a full flowing mane to keep it neat and tidy while you are riding.

ENDURANCE OR LONG-DISTANCE RIDING

▌ BELOW
The horse's weight is checked at the beginning and
end of the ride so that the amount of condition he
has lost can be judged.

There are two types of long-distance riding – competitive trail riding, and endurance riding. Trail riding is not a race but a test of your ability to have prepared your horse to complete a trail over a set course and distance and to present him at the end looking and feeling pretty much the same as he did when he set out. Your horse will have been thoroughly examined by a vet and judge before you set off and will be examined again half an hour after you complete the ride, which can be anything from 40–160km (25–100m). There is a set time in which to complete the trail and penalty points are awarded for finishing early or late. The horse that finishes in the best condition is the winner, but most competitors consider that 'to finish is to win'! Endurance riding IS a race – the winner being the first horse over the line who is judged to be 'fit to continue'. Endurance riding is an FEI sport and competitions are classified from one star to four star. Race distances vary from 80–160 km (50–100m). There are

The horse's pulse rate is monitored at intervals throughout a long-distance ride; the horse has to finish in good condition.

veterinary checks at the start, and at set points along the way (usually every 40km (25m)) as well as at the end. Most competitors and officials put the welfare of the horse first and foremost but sadly there has been some well-publicised cases of abuse, which has seen suspensions handed out to those concerned. The rules are in place to protect the horses that compete, but they will have to be obeyed and implemented at all levels for this sport to continue to thrive.

■ DEVELOPMENT OF THE SPORT

For many centuries the horse has been used to transport man and his possessions over great distances. Most countries can boast feats of great endurance riding – there has always been someone who has wanted to go further than those before him – but endurance riding as an organized competitive sport did not start in earnest until the 1950s.

Endurance riding today puts the horse's welfare first and foremost with strict veterinary checks. The organizers have the authority to eliminate any competitor whose horse shows signs of having had enough. Before this, some of the earliest long-distance races tested

the horse's endurance to the limit, with equine contestants literally being ridden until they dropped. The care and attention lavished on today's endurance horses is some recompense for the suffering endured by the horses who gave their all in previous centuries.

Interest in competitive endurance riding spread most quickly in Europe and America. The first endurance rides were actually organized to demonstrate the suitability of different types of horses as cavalry mounts. It was in California in 1955 that competitive endurance riding started. Interest was sparked by the ride

TACTICS

To succeed as an endurance rider you will need to be happy with your own company, have a good rapport with your horse and your back-up team, and an awareness of winning tactics. Who is ahead of you, who is behind you, are you keeping up with the pace, how can you avoid overtiring your horse, how can you help him if he does tire? What is your strategy at the checkpoints and the meeting points *en route* where your horse is allowed to rest? Whose horse can still put in a sprint for the finish, and how far ahead of them do you need to be to make sure you sprint over the line first?

▌ RIGHT
All kinds of natural hazards have to be tackled.

▌ BELOW
TREC riding is becoming an increasingly popular sport.

undertaken by Wendall T. Robie and a group of friends. They followed the old mining and emigrant trails over 100 miles (160 km) from Squaw Valley, through the Sierra Nevada range and on to Auburn. This trail became the world's first official endurance ride, and was named the Western States Trail Ride.

■ THE ENDURANCE HORSE

The main requirements of any endurance horse are that he has strong, dense bone, strong, healthy hooves, and a willingness and confidence to tackle whatever he is faced with because he will encounter all kinds of natural hazards on a long-distance ride. He should have a light, ground-covering action, and be balanced and sure-footed over all manner of terrain. He should be trained to settle into a steady trot or canter when required, and should accept a loose rein with minimal contact. A calm temperament means he will take less out of himself.

EQUIPMENT AND BACK-UP TEAM

Numnahs or gel pads are essential under saddles to reduce the risk of any rubbing or bruising, and purpose-designed endurance saddles can be purchased. Stock or Western-type saddles are popular as far as rider comfort is concerned. Many horses are ridden in hackamores (bitless bridles) to reduce the risk of sores or bruising, but these take practice and skill to use.

A good back-up team of between one and three helpers is essential during an endurance competition. They, as well as you, must be able to map read so that you all follow the same route and arrive at the same meeting points. They carry and provide everything that horse and rider may need along the way – food, water, clothing, spare tack (especially numnahs and girths, as these may need changing several times during a ride), spare horseshoes, a first-aid kit, a tack-repair kit, a torch, and a grooming kit and towels.

■ TREC

If endurance riding isn't quite for you, but the idea of exploring new countryside is, then TREC (Technique de Randonnee Equestre de Competition) may be just the thing. TREC originated in France as a way of improving and testing the skills of professional trekking guides but it soon became a popular international sport for all levels of horse and rider, and is another form of endurance riding with a fun element. It tests the rider's ability to plan and complete a long-distance ride in unknown country, and tests the horse's ability to cope with the obstacles he may meet along the way. There are three phases for riding competitors, and driving classes also, but they don't complete the third phase. Many of the skills required in the obstacle phase can be practised at home, or out and about hacking.

For the orienteering phase competitors follow a route on a map marked with the pace they must proceed at. There are random checkpoints along the way. Then there is an obstacle course of between one five kilometres. Some obstacles are tackled mounted and for others the horse is led. There may be water crossings, bridges, steps up and down, gates, low branches etc. Then riding competitors must show control of their horse's paces by cantering slowly along a marked narrow corridor (150m long/2–4m wide (490ft/6–12ft). The highest marks are given for the slowest canter and the fastest walk. It is a fun, enjoyable sport, open to all kinds of horses and ponies and is great for developing a true, trusting partnership.

WESTERN RIDING

Western riding is predominant in countries where the horse is still used to work cattle, such as America, Argentina, Australia, New Zealand and parts of Africa. It also has a growing following in other countries where riders are keen to enjoy the experience of riding a light, balanced, responsive horse, along with the novelty of trying many of the Western riding skills.

■ WHAT IS WESTERN RIDING?

America is the home of Western riding, which developed directly from the needs of the early pioneers. They depended on horses for their survival – for transport, for hunting food, and later for herding and managing vast herds of cattle. They had to be able to sit comfortably, for very long hours, in the saddle. They also needed horses who were both fast and responsive and yet also calm and easy to handle. The skills that horse and rider had to learn in order to earn a living in those times form the basis of the Western-riding competitions held today.

In Western riding you adopt a long leg position and carry the reins in one hand, leaving the other hand free to hold your gun or your lasso! The horse is controlled by the rider's weight and leg aids and by neck reining – responding to the pressure of the reins on his neck (see page 137). The Western horse is ridden on a long rein in a light and balanced manner. Western riding competitions test everything from the horse's ability to perform complex reining exercises and his skill at cutting out and controlling cattle, to his ability to weave his way through a line of barrels. There are World and European championships as well as numerous regional and national competitions.

■ ABOVE
In Western riding it is the seat and weight distribution of the rider that are used to control the horse, rather than the hand and leg as is usual in English riding.

■ LEFT
Western tack is designed to offer comfort, practicality and security to riders spending many hours in the saddle.

EQUIPMENT NEEDED

Many riders simply enjoy riding in the Western style – hacking or long-distance riding – without going as far as competing.

A Western or stock-type saddle adds authenticity and comfort to the proceedings but is not essential during the training of horse and rider. Similarly, a standard bridle and bit can be used, rather than the simpler Western-style bridle which may or may not be bitless. But once Western tack is used, no doubt you will want to be properly decked out too. Cowboy boots, which have a raised, supported instep and a higher heel than a standard riding boot, along with a pair of long, leather chaps are the two essentials.

■ RIGHT
In cattle-cutting competitions the horse has first to 'cut' a selected calf out from the rest of the herd, and then to prevent the selected animal from rejoining the herd. This Quarter Horse is using his own 'cattle sense' rather than his rider's instructions to keep the calf he is facing from joining the herd behind him.

■ THE WESTERN RIDING HORSE

Any horse can be converted to Western riding, but not all horses will have the temperament or inherent traits for all the Western-style competitions. The American Quarter Horse is a popular and successful choice – he has the speed, stamina, agility, intelligence and in-bred 'cattle sense' to succeed. Other American types, such as the Appaloosa, the Paint horse and the Pinto also feature strongly. But any horse with natural balance and agility, who can be taught to respond to weight and seat aids rather than being held between hand and leg as is usual in English-style riding, can be taught Western skills.

■ SKILLS REQUIRED

As a rider you must have good balance, the patience to build a rapport with your horse, which allows your commands to appear invisible to the onlooker and, if you are to become involved in cattle-handling skills, the overall fitness and toughness that these require. For most Western showing classes, the horse has to be taught the jog and the lope – these are basically a slow, smooth trot and canter. These gaits were developed for rider comfort and to reduce wear and tear on the horse's legs and joints. For most equestrian disciplines, the horse is trained to put spring and elevation into his paces, but for Western riding the paces are smooth and flat, with less knee and hock action than normal. Other classes require the horse to be taught various Western moves – the rollback, which is a fast 180° turn, the spin or pirouette, which is a 360° turn, the side pass (lateral work), the rein back, the sliding stop, and the flying change.

■ ABOVE In Western riding the horse is expected to be versatile and co-operative. At the Cowboy Ski Challenge in Jackson Hole, Wyoming, the horse demonstrates his ability to carry out any number of duties, from providing the power for the skiers...

RIGHT
The spin is one of the many Western skills that the horse has to learn.

SHOWING CLASSES

These are the easiest Western classes to train for and take part in.

■ The **Western Pleasure** class is the simplest. The horse is judged on how much of a pleasure he is to ride. He must work at all gaits on both reins, with the rider keeping the reins in one hand and a minimal contact. He is judged on how smooth his gaits and transitions are, and on how calm and responsive he is to his rider's commands.

■ The **Trail** class tests the horse's ability to cope calmly with the sorts of hazards he might encounter when riding the trail. There are a number of tasks you and he will have to perform in the ring, such as opening and closing a gate, backing through or around an obstacle, and jumping some logs. You may have to carry an object, and your horse may have to allow himself to be hobbled (tied up) on his own.

■ The **Western Riding** class imitates some of the tasks a ranch horse might have to carry out. The horse must demonstrate a good walk, jog and lope, and may have to tackle various tasks or

BELOW AND BELOW RIGHT
The sliding halt is one of the most dramatic Western-riding skills. The horse wears special skid boots to protect his fetlocks and to aid the slide.

obstacles similar to those also found in the trail class.

■ The **Reining** class tests some of the most advanced Western-riding techniques. The horse demonstrates at speed a pattern of various Western movements – turns, circles, spins, flying changes, rollbacks and sliding stops. All of these movements are performed from the lope – the slow, smooth canter.

CATTLE-HANDLING CLASSES

These require more extensive practice, training and facilities than the Western showing classes.

■ In the **Cutting Horse** class, the rider indicates to a judge which calf he is going to separate from the herd. The calf has to be 'cut out' from the herd and driven out into the arena. The rider must then adopt a loose rein and leave the job of preventing the calf from rejoining the herd to the horse. The cutting horse must be fast, athletic, brave and clever. The ability to outwit and outperform the calf is called 'cow sense' and is thought by many to be an inherited trait, rather than an acquired skill.

■ The **Working Cow Horse** class is judged in two sections: first the horse performs a reining pattern which demonstrates the

various Western movements, and then he has to hold, manoeuvre and control a cow within the arena, turning it several times as well as driving it along a fence line.

■ **Barrel Racing** is a fast, furious, grown-up version of that most popular of mounted games, the bending race! Horse and rider race around a course of barrels – they are allowed to touch the barrels but not to knock them over.

■ Other competitions, such as **Steer Wrestling** and **Calf Roping**, demonstrate and test the skills still required by the working cow pony and rider.

PRACTISING AT HOME

Western riding requires just as much practise and determination to improve as any other form of riding, and there is plenty you can practise at home.

■ BACK TO BASICS

Spend time perfecting the basics of your position and your horse's way of going. Watch the best riders to see how they hold their bodies, and how they work their horses. Achieving a balanced, secure position will allow you to help fulfill your horse's potential as you will be better able to teach him his job. Work on your horse to help him be relaxed, balanced, supple and responsive. These are the foundations that the more complicated manoeuvres are built upon.

▮ BELOW
Ask someone knowledgeable to watch you ride or ask someone to video you so that you can then compare yourself and your horse with the experts.

■ CATTLE HANDLING

If you are interested in taking part in cattle handling classes then you need to first introduce your horse to cattle. Stay relaxed yourself and help your horse to understand that although he must be quick and responsive, he must also stay calm and relaxed throughout this work. As you both become more accomplished you can start to work with larger cattle. Watch as many competitions and working cattle

handlers as you can and learn from them what works well and what doesn't. Then try putting the good things you have seen into practise on your own horse.

■ THE SLIDING HALT

This is one of the most spectacular reining movements, but it takes many months of correct training and practise to perform it correctly. The two main parts, the lope (canter) and the stop, have to be taught correctly and progressively. You can teach the horse the cue to stop by groundwork as well as ridden work. You want to achieve this with as little rein pressure as possible. So right from the start use the word 'Whoa' in a consistent way when asking him to stop when you are leading him or riding him – first in walk and then in trot. When riding, use consistent body aids also; as you say whoa, drop your weight into your heels and take your legs slightly

▮ LEFT
If your horse is young or inexperienced then start by introducing him to calves as they will be less intimidating than cattle.

away from the horse's sides, roll your seat bones under you and soften your lower back and pick up the reins. You want the horse to step actively into the halt by rounding his back and bringing his hindquarters under him.

Having perfected the stop aids you must also master a balanced relaxed lope. Practise this by working quietly up and down the arena, ensuring your horse remains straight through his body and remains straight on the line you are riding. Practise the stop from trot to start with, remembering to keep the horse balanced and straight as you apply the body and verbal aids that you have taught him.

▮ BELOW
When practising the sliding halt ensure the surface you are riding on is suitably soft. It will help the horse if you fit him with sliding plates (special flat shoes for his hind feet) when you are ready to try this in canter.

VAULTING

I **BELOW**
The team horse must maintain a consistent rhythm throughout all the exercises.

I **BOTTOM**
It takes a good athlete to maintain the grace, poise and balance of a gymnast while on a moving horse.

TThe sport of vaulting is a mixture of gymnastics and dance performed on a moving horse to music. Although it is now recognized as an international sport, governed by the FEI since 1982, it developed from an early teaching method that was used to accustom novice riders to the movement of the horse, and to instill a sense of balance and confidence.

Cavalry schools in particular used vaulting exercises to teach new recruits to develop their balance while the horse was in motion. Vaulting also served as a good fitness and strengthening exercise for riders, as well as giving them confidence when on horseback.

■ **SKILLS REQUIRED**

No riding experience is required but dance, martial arts, and gymnastic experience are good basic skills that will help you in this sport. You will need good natural balance, be naturally athletic and able to develop an air of grace and elegance. The sport also requires confidence – it takes a brave person to carry out many of the exercises with poise.

The horse needs to be quiet-natured, strong, unflappable and able to hold a steady, rhythmic, balanced canter on the lunge throughout the exercise.

The vaulter can practice many skills without his equine partner on a 'wooden horse' but most vaulters join a Vaulting club to develop their individual and team skills and routines.

■ **THE COMPETITIONS**

International vaulting competitions are made up of team, individual and pair classes. There are competitions for Seniors (over 16 yrs old), Juniors (14–18yrs old)

and Children (12–14 yrs old). A team comprises eight vaulters, one horse and one lunger, and a reserve vaulter. Both

the individual and the team competitions include a compulsory and a free-style test.

The horse works on the left rein only, mainly in canter on a 15m (49ft) circle.

There are two classes of international competition – CVI one star, and CVI two star. The World Championship is held every two years, and there are also intercontinental championships, including classes for all-male, all-female and mixed teams.

DISPLAY TEAMS

As well as taking part in competitions, vaulting teams are now often called upon to provide displays at shows and exhibitions. Such demonstrations are certainly an exciting, elegant and colourful way in which . to entertain a crowd of spectators.

PRACTISING AT HOME

As a vaulting athlete you will need to work on your general strength, and particularly your core strength, suppleness and balance. Practising yoga, which improves these three things, will be of great benefit also. It is important to warm up properly, stretching your muscles, before starting gymnastic or strengthening exercises. A 'wooden horse' to practice on can be made quite easily by using a large barrel and putting it on legs. You can strap a thick pad and vaulting surrface around this and practice your routines both on the ground and 'on the horse'.

■ FAR LEFT
Vaulting competitors need time to warm up in the same way as other gymnasts.

■ LEFT
The wooden horse is used for warming-up exercises as well as for practising set movements.

POLO

RIGHT
Polo originated in far hotter climates than these, but continues as a winter sport in St. Moritz

RIGHT
Polo originated in far hotter climates than these, but continues as a winter sport in St. Moritz

Of all the team ball games played on horseback, polo is the most widely played and recognized. The sport of polo carries an unashamedly glamorous image. It has always been expensive to take part in, mainly because of the string of ponies that is needed if you are to be a professional player. Despite the growing number of polo clubs, and the opportunities for children to learn to play provided by the Pony Club, polo remains an expensive sport, the greatest opportunities being open to the wealthy or the very talented.

Polo is thought to have originated in Persia about two-and-a-half thousand years ago. Its popularity spread to China, Japan, Tibet and Manipur, where British soldiers learned the game and wrote home about it. Soldiers in England started playing their own version based on the description they had been given, and British settlers took the game to Argentina. Polo is now played all over the world.

■ THE GAME
Polo is played on a grass or snow field 274m (901ft) long x 183m (600ft) wide. The field is framed with low boards to keep the ball in play, and there is a goal at each end. There are four players in a team, numbered as player one, two, three and four, and each has a specific role.

A full polo match is split into six seven-minute 'chukkas'. One pony can play a maximum of two chukkas but not consecutively. Each player uses a mallet to drive the ball down the field and into the opposition's goal. Obviously, the opposing team does its utmost to take possession of the ball and drive it the other way to score for themselves. All polo players are given a handicap ranging from -2 goals to +10 goals which represents their value to the team, it doesn't reflect how many goals he or she has scored. Teams are given an overall handicap value which dictates the level they may play at – high goal, medium, intermediate or low goal.

■ SKILLS REQUIRED
To succeed as a polo player you should be quick-thinking, fit, have very good co-ordination and balance, be physically and mentally tough and have good anticipation of how the game is going to proceed.

There are four main playing strokes to be mastered, as well as another eight subsidiary strokes. The four main strokes are the off-side forehander, off-side backhander, near-side forehander and near-side backhander. These strokes can be practised on a wooden horse as well as on your pony. Would-be players spend many hours simply 'stick and balling', i.e. cantering up and down a field, hitting a shot, chasing the ball and trying another stroke – up and down, around and around gradually getting a better result every time.

The rules of polo are quite complex and the game itself is fast moving, with the direction of play changing all the time. As a player you need to have an intimate understanding of the rules, as well as a continual awareness of where everyone is in relation to the direction of play.

EQUIPMENT NEEDED

To play polo you must be properly dressed – breeches, long boots, helmet with optional face guard, and knee protectors. You will also need your own polo mallets.

You must have at least two ponies – there is no longer a height restriction but polo mounts are still referred to as ponies. The rules insist that ponies wear standing martingales and that they have their tails tied up so that there is no risk of them becoming caught up in anything. The polo pony needs to be very fit, brave, responsive, quick-thinking, agile, fast and tough.

LEFT
Polo ponies have their legs protected by thick bandages during play.

HORSEBALL

Horseball is for those who enjoy a real contact sport – it resembles a cross between rugby football and basketball played on horseback. There are two teams of four players. The ball is about the size of a soccer ball and has leather loops sewn to it for handholds. The ball is thrown between the players and can be pulled from your opponents' hands, but if it drops to the ground it must be picked up without dismounting: riders have to bend down and scoop the ball up off the ground by grabbing hold of the leather loops. Whenever a rider is retrieving the ball off the ground, the other riders have to keep a distance as a safety precaution; otherwise they are offsides. The stirrups are tied together under the horse's belly, making it easier for the rider to reach down.

A goal is scored by throwing the ball through a suspended loop that has a net attached to it. The game is started, and restarted after a goal, by a throw-in similar to that used in rugby. The ball is tossed in the air between two riders who each strive to grab it first. The game can be played

■ LEFT
Horseball has grown rapidly in popularity in recent years, as a game for both adults and children.

■ BELOW LEFT
The ball is moved rapidly down the arena towards the goal. In order to score, the ball has to be thrown through a high loop with a net attached.

EQUIPMENT NEEDED

The joy of playing horseball is that the equipment required for the sport is cheap and simple. The ball can be made by having leather loops sewn to a normal soccer ball and the goal can be made from a kind of post, using a hoop and a net. If you are going to play bareback, whoever sews the loops to your ball can also be asked to sew handholds to a surcingle, which will hold a numnah in place on the horse's back and give you some security.

indoors or outdoors, and is a sport enjoyed by both adults and children.

Because the ball can only travel as far and as fast as you can throw it, horseball does not require the same speed from its contestants as, say, polo. For this reason any horse or pony who is well behaved in company, i.e. can be trusted not to kick or nip an opposing pony or rider, and who is reasonably well schooled, can be introduced to the game.

The greatest advantage of horseball is that, because the equipment is relatively cheap and easy to make, it is ideal as a fun, impromptu game for a group of friends on horseback. At the other extreme it can be played fast, furious and mean by teams with their hearts set on regional and national championship glory.

PONY CLUB HORSEBALL

The Pony Club adopted the game with enthusiasm, as the organizers could see its potential as a fun way of improving riding skills and confidence. To make it additionally beneficial as a training exercise, at Pony Club level horseball is played bareback. You sit on a numnah held in place with a surcingle which has two handholds. When you have to reach down to scoop the ball off the ground, you can use the handholds to help keep your balance. To ensure that the ponies don't get pulled in the mouth, you have to drop the reins when you catch the ball.

POLOCROSSE

■ LEFT AND BELOW
Ponies and riders need to be athletic and versatile, as well as unflappable!

Polocrosse is based on the mounted game of polo and on lacrosse, a ball game that is played on foot. While polo originated in the Far East and lacrosse in North America, both were introduced to Europe by returning servicemen and travellers. Polocrosse was first played in 1932 in London. It was used as an exercise to encourage better riding skills and was originally played by teams of two, indoors. It quickly developed into a four-man team

EQUIPMENT AND SKILLS NEEDED

To play polocrosse you need one horse and a polocrosse racket. The only other necessary equipment is protective boots and bandages for your horse's legs. All kinds of horses and ponies play the game, from Shetland ponies to thoroughbreds, making it a good family game. You need to have a safe and secure seat in the saddle; beyond that, it is just a case of practicing your catching and throwing skills, which can be done on the ground as well as mounted.

outdoor game. In 1938, an Australian couple who watched the game in England took the idea back home with them to Australia, where it became the fast and exciting game that it is today. Polocrosse is played in many different countries around the world, and there are numerous inter-club championships as well as a World Championship.

■ THE GAME

Polocrosse is played between two teams of six, all of whom are equipped with a long-handled racket that has a net on the end of it. A soft rubber ball is the object of play; it is caught in the net of the racket and passed between players by throwing or bouncing it.

The game is split into six chukkas, each lasting for eight minutes. Each team is divided into two and they alternate for

each chukka so that only three of the six team members are on the field at one time. The game is played on a large area slightly bigger than a rugby field. The field is divided by penalty lines over which the ball must not be carried – the player must either bounce and retrieve it, or throw it to a teammate.

There is a goal at each end consisting of two poles 8 feet (2.5 m) apart. The ball must be thrown between these in order to score. Only the Number One player is allowed to shoot at goal. The defending Number Three player is allowed in the goal-scoring area to protect the goal and to tackle the attacking Number One. The Number Two players are only allowed in the midfield area.

■ BELOW
Many younger riders are introduced to team ball games on horseback by the Pony Club. Polocrosse is a popular alternative to polo, although the Pony Club fields many high-quality polo teams as well.

PRACTISING AT HOME

As Polo, Polocrosse and Horseball are all team sports, most practise sessions take place at a club which will have suitable grounds to practise and play on. But there is plenty you can work on at home. Schooling your horse to be as balanced, supple and responsive as possible will make the sport easier for both of you, so incorporating the correct principles of flatwork whilst working your horse will pay dividends.

■ NECK REINING

Even if your chosen pastime with your horse or pony doesn't require either of you to be expert at neck reining, it is a skill worth teaching and practising as, inevitably, there will be occasions when you have to control your horse with only one hand on the reins, such as for opening and closing gates. But for a number of horse sports, including polo and polocrosse, it is an essential requirement.

■ LEFT
Practice makes perfect. Even the most complex shots can be practised without getting on a horse – at least not a real one.

1 Start by turning your horse to the left as you would normally – take the left rein out wide so that you are drawing the horse to the left, and bring your right rein over the horse's neck so that you are applying rein pressure to the right hand side of his neck. Use your inside leg on the girth as you would normally, and control the swing of the quarters by keeping your outside leg behind the girth. Turn your hips and upper body to the left.

2 Continue practising this but gradually reduce the degree to which you use your left hand to draw the horse to the left, and concentrate more on applying pressure to the horse's neck with the right rein. Use your legs and upper body position to help guide the horse also. Once you feel the horse responding to the neck rein aid, put both reins in one hand to make the turn.

3 Apply the same technique on the other rein; the right hand draws the horse to the right, left hand brings the left rein over the neck to apply pressure to the neck, right leg on the girth, left leg behind the girth and upper body turned to the right. Your horse will soon learn to respond to the movement of your legs and body, and the lightest touch with the reins on the neck.

Driving

Horses and ponies are well designed for the task of pulling a vehicle of some kind or other. Remember that a horse has to be taught how to rearrange his balance and posture in order to carry a rider, whereas pulling something comes more naturally.

Driving is a lot of fun – although many riders find it more nerve-racking than riding – and it can be undertaken in as simple or elaborate a way as desire and finances allow.

■ DRIVING FOR PLEASURE

Many a family pony has been converted from riding to driving once the children have outgrown him. Given a patient and common-sense approach, most horses and ponies of an equable nature will convert to driving; many even show a preference for it, though there are always exceptions.

The first stage in training a driving horse is to accustom him to wearing blinkers. He should be lunged and long reined in these, and finally hacked out in them. After that, introduce him to the rest of the harness. The next stage involves

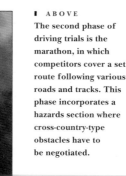

getting him to pull something safe, such as an old tyre. It is not the weight of what he is pulling that is likely to bother him, but his awareness of something following behind him and the noise it makes. Once he is comfortable with this he is well on the way to being introduced to a simple cart of some sort. Straightforward as it all sounds, experienced help should always be sought in the training process.

Driving clubs will provide a social dimension to a leisure activity that can otherwise be quite a solitary one.

■ COMPETITION DRIVING

The world of competition driving revolves around the show ring and driving trials. Show-ring driving follows a similar format to ridden showing classes; driving trials resemble ridden horse trials and consist of three disciplines – a dressage test, a marathon and an obstacle competition.

In show-ring driving, the full turnout of horse or pony, his harness, the cart, the furnishings and the appearance of the driver and groom are all judged, as well as the behaviour and way of going of the whole team. Competing in driving trials requires far more time, practice and equipment than show-ring driving.

Harness racing, which involves specially bred trotters or pacers pulling a lightweight racing cart, is another specialty sport that attracts a great spectator following. The horses can travel at a tremendous speed at the trot, and race each other around an oval track.

▮ ABOVE
The second phase of driving trials is the marathon, in which competitors cover a set route following various roads and tracks. This phase incorporates a hazards section where cross-country-type obstacles have to be negotiated.

▮ LEFT
In show-ring driving the overall turnout and performance of the competitors is judged. This smart little Welsh mountain pony is creating a good all-around impression in the ring.

▮ OPPOSITE
For competition purposes,
a team of four is about as
complicated as you want to
get, but horses can be driven
in larger teams than this.

▮ BELOW
Driving horses and ponies, and the
vehicles they pull, come in all manner
of shapes and sizes, and can be driven
in different ways. This pair of ponies
is being driven abreast.

▮ BELOW
Driving a pair in tandem (one behind
the other) makes it far more difficult
to negotiate the complex obstacles
because of the additional length of
the horses and carriage.

The necessary equipment is relatively
inexpensive, as the carts are lightweight
and basic in design, but it is a fiercely
competitive sport.

SHOW-RING DRIVING CLASSES

▮ In **Private Driving** classes the
competitors may be sent off for a drive
around the surrounding roads with the
judge following in a car to see how they
react and behave.

▮ **Light Trade** classes are for horse-drawn
vehicles that were, or still are, used for
trade purposes, such as deliveries of
goods. An additional requirement in these
classes is for the horses to stand still
unattended, which they would have to do
while their goods were being unloaded.

▮ The **Concour d'Elegance** class is judged
more on overall poise than on close detail.

▮ **Scurry Driving** is a popular class at many
British shows. Pairs of ponies, which must
be either 12hh and under, or between
12hh and 14.2hh, are harnessed to small,
four-wheeled vehicles carrying a driver
and groom. They race around an obstacle
course marked out by cones, which
involves tight turns and high speeds and a
lot of noise from the spectators. Any cones
knocked over are penalized by adding
extra seconds to the overall race time.
The groom has to play a very active role –

leaning out to either side to help maintain
the vehicle's balance as it swings around
the corners.

▮ Additional show-ring classes include the
likes of **Drive and Ride** competitions and
Heavy Horse classes. There may also be
the opportunity to put on a display to
entertain the public.

DRIVING TRIALS

▮ For the first phase, you have to perform
a simple dressage test within the confines
of a large arena; this is given a score based

Water is a popular hazard in driving trials. This pair
of ponies is negotiating a simple water crossing with
great enthusiasm.

on the performance and on the overall
presentation.

▮ The marathon, which comes next,
involves covering approximately 15½ miles
(25 km) in about two hours. There are
five different sections and two compulsory
ten-minute breaks.

– The first section can be completed at
any gait but trotting is usually sufficient to
make the time.

– The second section must be
performed at a walk and is followed by
a ten-minute rest.

– The third section usually involves
a stretch of more arduous terrain, and a
fast trot is required to make the time;
cantering is not allowed.

– The fourth section is another walk
section, followed by a ten-minute break.

– With the fifth section the excitement
really begins. This involves negotiating
various man-made or natural hazards at
speed, as this section is timed.

▮ The final phase is the obstacle or cone-
driving competition. This tests the horses'
obedience and the driver's ability to drive
accurately between sets of cones that
mark out the course. Once again, this
section is timed.

▮ The overall winner is the one with the
best combined score over the three
different phases.

Jumping Sports

Jumping requires confidence, rhythm and balance. Once you have a fair degree of these three skills you can start to discover the world of jumping sports. Show jumping offers competitions for fun as well as for fortune seekers, and provides an excellent and safe way to practise your jumping skills and gain experience. Once you feel confident about show jumps – which fall down if you hit them – you may want to try your hand at jumping solid obstacles. Hunting and hunter trials provide you with the opportunity to do this – and when you are feeling confident enough you can progress to team chasing or eventing. For the brave and robust there is race riding – the ultimate way to jump at speed.

HUNTING

There is little to beat the exhilaration of riding fast across country. You and your horse must tackle whatever is thrown in your way while looking eagerly ahead for the next challenge.

The thrill of the chase as experienced when hunting on horseback usually succeeds in lifting the spirits of all horsemen and women. Hunting, for many, provides an opportunity to tackle much greater challenges than they might otherwise contemplate.

■ HUNTING LAWS IN THE UK

Hunting has created a lengthy social debate between anti-hunting protesters, who argue the sport is cruel and barbaric, and pro-hunters, who argue that hunting on horseback is a valuable country sport, contributing to the conservation of the countryside and management of wildlife.

▌ ABOVE
Hunting etiquette requires that you and your mount are smartly and tidily turned out. Your horse's or pony's mane should be plaited (braided), your tack should be gleaming, and you should be turned out in clean jodhpurs, boots and jacket.

▌ BELOW
The hounds are controlled by a huntsman; he is usually assisted by a whipper-in who helps to keep the hounds together as a pack.

After many attempts by members of Parliament to ban hunting through private members' bills in the UK, the Hunting Act 2004 was passed in that year, resulting in the outlawing of hunting with hounds.

The eventual law resulted in acts such as fox hunting, organized hare coursing, hunting deer, hares and mink with large groups of hounds becoming illegal. However, flushing quarry with no more than two dogs and shooting the quarry dead in order to prevent it causing serious damage to the environment and other wildlife or domestic animals is still allowed. Hunting organizations such as the Countryside Alliance continue to oppose the Act, claiming it is confusing and hard to follow. Ironically, since the ban, hunting in its new form has gained ever increasing support from new participants.

❚ LEFT
You are never too young or too old to go hunting.
Many children are taken out, and an abundance of
youthful seniors still hunt regularly.

Drag hunting and hunting with bloodhounds, to find and follow a scent, is still legal in England and Wales. In Scotland, flushing quarry by packs of dogs, in order to be shot, is still allowed under the Protection of Wild Mammals (Scotland) Act 2002. In Northern Ireland, hunting is legal.

■ DIFFERENT TYPES OF HUNTING

HUNTING QUARRY

Over the centuries various animals have been hunted from horseback in many parts of the world. The most common ones in recent times are the fox and stag in England and Ireland, the wild boar in other parts of Europe, and the coyote in North America and parts of Africa. The hunting of any of these animals relies on the co-operation and permission of the landowners whose property is crossed.

In some countries packs of hounds are bred and trained to pick up the scent and track down the hunted animal. The hounds are usually controlled by a huntsman who is the person responsible for the hounds. The hunt followers, or field as they are often known, are sometimes helpful in observing the whereabouts of the hounds or the direction the hunted quarry has taken, but their main role is to help pay for the upkeep of the hunt's hounds, horses and hunting country. In return for an annual subscription and a 'cap' – an additional donation to hunt funds made on the day of the hunt – the hunt follower enjoys seeing hounds at work and the thrill of the chase.

The field follow the huntsman who heads off first with the hounds to pick up the scent. Leading the field is the field master whose instructions you must obey at all times – and who you should avoid overtaking! Some days are good scenting days and the hounds can easily follow the scent; other days are not so good.

Once the hounds are on the scent of their quarry, they will follow it across all manner of country. The mounted followers keep up as best they can, the bravest and most talented jumping everything in their path, the rest finding a way around the edges of fields, through gates and along tracks. A good knowledge of the local countryside helps in the task of keeping up with the hounds. If you are crossing country that has been planted with crops, only the hounds and huntsman are allowed to take the direct line after the prey. The field have to find a way round which minimizes any damage to the crops; an intimate knowledge of your surroundings makes this easier. Etiquette demands that you follow the lead of the field master, but after a good run behind hounds the field often gets split up and strung out, and it is up to you to find the hounds again.

The hounds will either succeed in catching their prey or they will lose track of it, or may have to be called off if the fox crosses land that the hunt doesn't have

❚ LEFT
Whether you are hunting foxes, coyote, rabbit, or with drag or bloodhounds, nothing very exciting happens until the hounds pick up the appropriate scent and set off.

▌ LEFT
**At the end of a long, hard day's hunting the field is
greatly diminished. It is one of the most satisfying
feelings in the world to be among the few left at the
end of the day.**

permission to cross. In any case the
hounds are taken to another cover to see
if they can pick up the scent of another
fox, and so it goes on.

Most hunt meets are organized for
mid-morning, and hunting continues until
late afternoon. At about lunchtime
'second horses' are arranged. This means
that the huntsman and the master will
change on to fresh horses who have been
brought by lorry to a pre-arranged point.
Their first horses are taken home, washed
and dried off, rugged up, fed and stabled.
Hunt followers may also change on to
second horses if they have another horse
and have been able to organize someone
to deliver it.

DRAG HUNTING

This involves a pack of hounds and
mounted followers but, instead of hunting
a live quarry, the hounds follow a trail
that has been laid earlier in the day by
someone dragging a bag laced with a
strong scent that the hounds have been
taught to pick up and follow. This is now
the only legal form of hunting with a pack
of hounds in England, Wales and Scotland.

Drag hunting gives you the chance to
ride fast across country, behind hounds.
It is safer and more predictable than
hunting live quarry because you are
following a pre-set course. The jumps will
be either safe, natural features or man-
made fences. A knowledge of the country

is not necessary as the course the hounds
take is pre-determined. Many hunts offer
days specifically for the novice or nervous,
when they will make sure the jumps
encountered are smaller than usual.

Subscriptions from the field help to pay
for the upkeep of the hounds and kennels.

BLOODHOUNDS

Hunting with bloodhounds is another
form of drag hunting. This time the
hounds are following the scent of a man
who sets off some time before the hunt
starts. The runner will follow a previously
agreed trail, making this form of hunting
as safe as drag hunting. The bloodhounds
are very friendly and will not harm their
'prey' when they catch up with him!

■ SKILLS REQUIRED

Hunting suits all types of horse and pony –
it seems to inspire the less cautious to be
even braver, but it can also cause a great
deal of over-excitement. It is important to
have developed a reasonably strong and
secure seat and to be able to balance your
horse in order to help him tackle the

EQUIPMENT NEEDED

Your horse should be well turned out with his mane
plaited (braided). He will need a good, strong set of
tack, as a good-quality saddle and bridle will add to
your own safety. Hunting entails long hours in the
saddle, often in bad weather conditions. The last
thing you want is for a rein or stirrup leather to snap
when you are in the middle of nowhere, riding at a
flat-out gallop and heading for a large and solid
post-and-rail fence!

Put an especially well-padded numnah under the
saddle to make it more comfortable for the horse
and to reduce the risk of him being rubbed.

Whether or not your horse wears boots to protect
his legs is a matter of personal choice. Your horse's
legs are at great risk of being knocked or scratched
out hunting, but many boots, once they are wet and
muddy and have been worn for several hours, start
to rub anyway. You will need to decide which is the
lesser of two evils.

As a rider you are expected to be smartly turned
out. You should wear traditional-coloured breeches
or jodphurs, teamed with either long riding boots
or short jodhpur boots. You must wear either a
hacking jacket (tweed jacket) or a plain blue or black
jacket. A helmet with blue or black velvet silk should
be worn and this should have a well-fitting safety
harness. If you wear a hacking jacket it is correct to
wear a shirt and coloured stock (similar to a cravat or
broad neck tie) held in place with a stock pin. A plain
cream or white stock should be worn with a blue or
black jacket. A body protector may be worn also.

Gloves should be worn and a stick carried. You
should carry in your pockets some good, thick
string, such as baling twine, and a folding penknife
(jackknife) so that you can help make repairs to any
gates or fences that get broken by the less able
jumpers in the field. A day's hunting can end up
being a very long day – find room in your pockets

for a couple of sandwiches or a bar of chocolate to
keep you going.

If you are going to hunt a lot, a hunting whip and a
pair of wire cutters are worth buying. A hunting whip
is a shaped cane with a long leather lash on the end.
The cane is useful for helping you to open and shut
gates, and the lash, if let down so that it hangs by
your horse's legs, can be used to prevent hounds
from going right underneath your horse where they
are more likely to get kicked or trampled.

A leather carrying pouch can be fitted to your
saddle in which you can keep a pair of wire cutters.
No matter how diligent you are, when you are
crossing unknown country it is possible to get caught
up in one of the hazards of agriculture – wire netting
or barbed wire. It is therefore invaluable to have a
pair of wire cutters for cutting your own horse free or
for helping anyone else unfortunate enough to be
caught out.

BELOW
Ladies traditionally only rode side-saddle, and the elegant picture it creates is one reason for a growing number of people returning to the habit.

varied terrain and obstacles that you will encounter during the hunt. Whether you are riding around a cross-country course or are genuinely crossing the country out hunting, the approach to jumping is the same: keep the horse well balanced and in a good rhythm. Keep in contact with the horse with your legs, seat and hands so that you can help balance him as he negotiates the unexpected. Consider the experience and ability of yourself and your horse when deciding when to jump and when to find a way round. When you do jump, give your horse room to see what he has to do, remember that the horses around you may run out, fall or refuse so keep your wits about you.

Your horse needs to be fit, as he will be required to gallop and jump, often with little chance to rest. He should be well mannered; he must accept other horses all around him. If you have even the slightest suspicion that he may panic or kick out, keep him out of the crowd. It is your responsibility to prevent your horse from hurting anyone else. A young or

inexperienced horse should be introduced quietly to the hunting field. It is often a good idea to avoid the first hour of the meet when all the horses are fresh and excited, and perhaps join the hunt later in the day. Keep the horse moving and thinking forwards but do not allow him to get caught up in the crush of the field until he is used to all the sights and sounds. It is considered an unforgiveable sin to let your horse kick a hound, so be constantly aware of where the hounds are in relation to your horse. Keep his hindquarters turned away from the hounds if they approach or pass by you.

In the excitement of the chase do not overlook your horse's well-being. Keep in mind how tired he might be. His own adrenalin from the excitement will make

him think he can do more than perhaps he really can, so do not keep him out too long to start with, until you have a clearer idea of his real fitness. Think responsibly about what you ask him to jump. Never be tempted to jump wire – find a gate instead. Look out too for hazards such as rabbit holes and discarded farm machinery.

■ NEGOTIATING GATES
Opening and closing gates is a valuable skill to acquire. Whether you are just out hacking, or hunting or hunter trialling, a great deal of time and trouble can be saved if you can open and close gates from the back of your horse. Never underestimate the risk of getting caught in the gate, or your tack or clothing getting hooked up on the latch. Weigh up the risks before deciding whether to tackle the gate from the back of your horse or from the ground. As mentioned previously, teaching your horse to neck rein (see page 137) will make tasks such as this so much easier, along with teaching him to rein back (reverse, see pages 50 – 51).

1 Ride up to the gate, put your reins and stick in one hand and lean forward to unlatch the gate. If room, position your horse side-on to the gate. If not, you will have to quietly ride him up to the gate and he will put his head over it.

2 If the gate opens towards you, then your horse will need to rein back while you pull the gate open towards you. If it opens the other way, it is easiest if you can push the gate firmly away from you. Or ride your horse quietly forwards whilst pushing the gate ahead of you.

3 Be sure there is enough room to pass through the opening safely. Do not risk your horse or your leg getting banged against the gate post. To close the gate, you will have to go through the whole procedure in reverse. Be sure the latch is definitely fastened before riding away.

HUNTER TRIALS AND TEAM CHASING

For those who want to be judged on their cross-country riding skills, there is the option of competing in hunter trials and team chases. In a hunter trial you may ride the course as an individual or as one of a pair. In team chasing there are four team members to motivate each other.

In hunter trials you are expected to tackle a course of cross-country fences, the height of which varies depending on the class you enter. Some competitions cater for leading-rein riders, others offer a range of classes with fences varying from about 2 ft 6 in to 3 ft 9 in (0.75–1.2 m). The organizers decide upon an optimum time, which is based on horse and rider tackling the course at what is commonly described as a fair hunting pace. Within the course there is usually an additional timed section that often includes a gate that has to be opened and shut – not jumped! The winners are the horse and rider who jump clear and complete the course nearest to the optimum time – which is not revealed to the riders until after the competition. If more than one rider finishes on the optimum time, the winner is the fastest one through the timed section.

◼ ABOVE
Water is one of the most common problems encountered at a hunter trial. There is no reason why it should be feared provided it is introduced quietly and calmly. This pony looks a bit tentative and needs to gain more confidence before he is likely to tackle water with enthusiasm.

◼ BELOW LEFT
Hunter trials offer a huge variety of challenges for all ages and abilities. Even lead-line riders can take part, provided their helpers are as agile as their ponies!

◼ SKILLS REQUIRED

A good cross-country horse needs to enjoy what he is doing and provided you have introduced your horse to cross-country obstacles in a calm, progressive way, then there is no reason why he shouldn't enjoy himself. He should allow you to ride him in a controllable, balanced rhythm across varying terrain and will need to have developed a tidy jumping technique so

◼ LEFT
Cross-country riding is Competing as a pair is a good way of introducing an inexperienced or nervous horse or rider to the thrill of cross-country riding, as they can gain confidence from their partners.

BELOW
This horse and rider have both taken a good soaking at the water hazard, but the joy of team chasing is that, provided the rest of the team got through, there is still a chance of winning. It just means there is a little consolation for the faller – his team will have galloped away into the distance!

BELOW
Team chasing involves a team of four riding fast and furiously across country. The competition is based on the time it takes for the first three team members to complete the course.

accurately and safely to start with. This practice exercise is based on a gymkhana game called Chase Me Charlie. In this game, the team players all follow each other over a single jump in the arena. If you knock the fence down, you are out! After everyone has jumped, the fence is raised and all those left in go again. The game continues until you are left with a winner – which will be the only one to clear the final fence.

that he can safely negotiate solid obstacles. As a rider you will need to have good balance, a secure seat and strong lower leg so you can give your horse the confidence to keep going forwards to tackle whatever obstacles and hazards come your way. For the timed section, where you will have to open and close a gate, your horse must be responsive to your aids so that you can ask him to rein-back, or move sideways to the left or right, in order that you can carry out this task as quickly as possible. You will need to develop a good sense of speed, and the ability to keep your horse balanced at that speed, so that you can get as close to the optimum time as possible, whilst still jumping safely.

EQUIPMENT NEEDED

To compete in a hunter trial you need to be turned out in your hunting attire, although most organizers allow you to wear a sweat shirt or polo shirt instead of a jacket. They will, however, insist that you wear a proper safety helmet and harness, as well as a body protector.

Your horse will need his usual saddle and bridle, as long as these are clean and in good condition, and his legs should be protected with either boots or bandages.

A normal riding stick or hunting whip may be carried; for hunter trials a proper hunting whip may help in opening and shutting the gate quickly in the timed section.

■ TEAM CHASING

Team chases are held over a variety of different-sized cross-country courses. Teams of four riders set off around the course, and progress is timed from the moment a team sets off to the moment the third rider crosses the line. So if one member of your team is left behind you still have a chance of winning.

The winning team is the one whose first three riders complete the course in the fastest time. Penalties are not given for falls or refusals – it is all judged on speed. For this reason the number of falls can be quite high. If the lead horse falls and the others are coming too fast and too close behind, at least one other member of the team is likely to fall also. But there is never any need to give up hope – even if one of the team stops or falls, provided the team can make up time somewhere else they still have a chance at placing. Regional and national championships are held.

■ PRACTISING AT HOME

You can help your horse get used to the idea of team chasing and pairs hunter trials by practising in an arena over show jumps. This is safer than practising over solid cross-country fences until your horse is used to jumping in company. Some horses settle very quickly to the idea of jumping with another horse, others become over-excited or distracted and may not concentrate on jumping

1 For team chase or pairs practice you can set up a small fence and follow each other over it. If your horse is excited, try to concentrate on maintaining the same rhythm on the circle and make the jump part of your circle. Keep a good distance apart to start with. As both horses settle to the idea, you can follow more closely behind one another.

2 Swap over so that the lead horse now follows the other horse. Again, give both horses time to settle to the idea and when they are both concentrating on their jumping you can get closer together and make the jump higher. You can practice passing each other so that the lead horse changes each time you jump the jump. If you have space to make the fence wide enough you can practise jumping it side by side.

SHOW JUMPING

The sport of show jumping involves tackling a course of artificial jumps, as opposed to natural cross-country jumps. It takes place in an arena that can be grass or have an all-weather surface, indoors or outdoors. An Olympic sport governed by the FEI, it is also a popular unaffiliated sport with any number of classes being held at local shows.

Show jumping requires accuracy and care. Almost every horse or pony can jump, but they do not all have the technique or the will to clear the fences.

Show jumping developed from the 'leaping competitions' that were held at various shows in Europe and America during the late nineteenth century. There were high-jump and long-jump competitions for horse and rider, but the idea of jumping a course of fences was, at the time, mainly restricted to natural cross-country fences. Jumping was first included in the Olympic Games in Paris in

■ LEFT
Teaching your horse to go well on the flat is as important to his success as teaching him how to jump correctly; look at the beautifully round and elevated canter that this show jumper is producing – with a canter like this, jumping the fence is almost a formality.

1900. It incorporated the high and wide competitions plus a timed competition over a course of artificial show jumps. In 1907, the first International Horse Show was held at Olympia in London, England, and the show jumping proved to be very popular. From then on competitions were organized throughout Europe and America for major trophies such as the Nations Cup. This began as a military competition open to three officers of the same nationality who had to compete in uniform. Today it is open to four riders of the same nationality, male or female, military or civilian.

■ SHOW JUMPING COMPETITIONS

The simplest form of unaffiliated competition is the Clear Round Class, held at any number of local shows. This is an excellent way of introducing an inexperienced horse and rider to the sport. Each rider pays a small fee to tackle a course of jumps. If you jump a clear round you win a ribbon, but the real usefulness of the competition is that if you jump a fence badly you can turn around and jump it again. Most organizers of these classes are extremely tolerant and will even lower a fence for you if your

■ BELOW
If you can invest in a few jumps of your own, or team up with some friends to share them, there is much that can be practised at home. A simple thing to practise is always looking toward the next fence. This helps you to judge your turns and your approach. Once you have taken off over a fence you should be looking toward your next target; as you ride around the course you should always be looking toward where you have to go next.

EQUIPMENT NEEDED

To develop your show-jumping skills you need to have access to at least three or four sets of jump standards and poles. Other than that, all that is needed is a reasonably flat surface to practise on, which can be a grass paddock when ground conditions permit, or an outdoor or indoor arena with an all-weather surface. Your horse needs only his usual saddle and bridle and should wear protective boots of some sort. Most show jumpers use open-fronted boots on the front legs so that the tendon area is protected but the horse will feel the knock if he hits a pole, and short fetlock boots behind. At smaller shows you may wear riding boots and chaps, jodhpurs or breeches. At higher level shows, proper show attire is required.

■ RIGHT
Riders all develop their own jumping style as they gain confidence and experience, but one of the things you must always do, no matter what your technique, is to ensure that you give your horse plenty of freedom of his head and neck. Your hands must always move forward when the horse is jumping over the fence.

jumpers, or for added entertainment they may build two identical courses side by side over which competitors race. Time faults are added for knock-downs.

American jumping classes are split between hunters, jumpers and equitation classes. In hunter classes the round is judged on the style and technique of both horse and rider, as well as their actual performance. Jumper classes are judged on penalties for jumping errors and time, as in standard showjumping classes. Equitation classes are judged on the rider's ability, style and technique.

■ SKILLS REQUIRED
Flatwork training is as important to the show jumper as jump schooling. A balanced, rhythmic and elevated canter is essential if the horse is to jump successfully. Whatever it is you are jumping, your chances of clearing it safely are mainly reliant on how good an approach you give the horse to the fence. The horse must be able to negotiate corners and turns while still keeping his rhythm and balance, so he needs to be supple and responsive.

horse continually refuses. In a proper competition you would be eliminated after three refusals.

The next stage is the two-round competition. Each competitor tackles the same course of fences and if you jump a clear round you go through to the jump off. This is ridden against the clock and the fastest clear round wins.

Fences in unaffiliated classes start as low as the organizer wishes. There may even be beginner classes with jumps only 18 inches (45 cm) high. Fences usually go up to about 3 feet 11 inches (1.2 m). Affiliated competitions start with a novice class with fences from about 3 feet (90 cm) high and continue through the levels to courses with jumps that are well over 6 feet (1.8 m) high.

There are also other types of jumping classes such as 'Gambler's Choice'. This involves a course of fences that each have a different value in terms of points to be won. You jump as many fences as you can in the time allowed, in any order you like, with the aim of accumulating the maximum number of points. The *Puissance* involves jumping a short course

of fences; these include a wall, which is always the highest jump. The fences are gradually raised until nobody is able to clear the wall.

Derby competitions have cross-country-type obstacles in the arena, such as banks and ditches. Some shows also hold relay competitions between teams of show

■ LEFT
This little pony is showing superb technique – see how tightly he has snapped up and folded his front legs, which gives him every chance to clear the fence.

As a rider you will need to understand how to train your horse to improve his jumping technique, as well as your own ability to maintain the horse's balance and rhythm between fences. Gridwork can be used to improve overall gymnastic ability as well as to enhance technique and the shape the horse makes over a fence. The grid can also be set up to encourage the horse to shorten or lengthen his stride. The ability of horse and rider to be able to lengthen or shorten the stride depending on the challenge set by the course designer is essential to safely negotiate combinations and related distances.

Some riders – and horses – are blessed with a natural ability to gauge distances and to know immediately whether they need to lengthen or shorten their stride to meet the next fence successfully. But every rider can develop this skill by practising riding different distances between fences at home and getting a feel for the type of canter they need to be in to cover long or short distances between fences. Patience and consistency in training, and a cool head and confidence at home and at a competition are skills which will stand any competitor in good stead.

■ **LEFT**
Show-jumping competitions usually just involve jumping over fences. However, in Derby classes cross-country type obstacles are introduced; this is the world-famous Hickstead Derby bank.

■ **BELOW**
In show jumping the horse has to be taught to jump *over* water, whereas in cross-country riding you are always trying to encourage your horse to jump *into* water.

■ **OPPORTUNITIES**
In all sports there are those who compete purely for their own enjoyment and entertainment, and those who compete with a view to being selected for team competitions and, who knows, maybe ultimately the Olympics. Show jumping caters extremely well to both types of competitor. For the less ambitious there are no end of unaffiliated and affiliated classes and competitions that still allow horse and rider to progress through the levels. They can go as far as their ability, time and/or finances allow them.

For those looking for greater rewards, show jumping also offers very good opportunities. Through the FEI there is a training and team-selection programme for pony riders, juniors, young riders and seniors. There are also Pony Club and riding club competitions and championships. To be considered for team selection usually involves informing the appropriate selection committee of your interest and then entering a number of specified competitions where your performance will be noted by the selectors. If you are a likely candidate for a team place, you may be invited to attend various training courses – but remember that the ability to operate as part of a team is as important as being a good enough competitor to warrant selection.

PRACTISING AT HOME

A successful show-jumping round is very much down to being able to maintain a good balance and rhythm in the canter as you make your way around the course. You can practise this at home by trying a couple of simple exercises.

■ CIRCLE EXERCISE

Place four poles on the ground so that they are evenly spaced out around a large 20 or 25m (65 to 82ft) circle.

1 Start by trotting over the poles, concentrating on keeping an even rhythm and balance and a consistent and correct bend through the horse's body. Do not anticipate the poles, but allow the horse to concentrate on those while you concentrate on the rhythm, balance and bend. Keep your eye up and look ahead to the middle of each pole so that you stay on an accurate circle.

2 Once you have got the feel of this in trot, you can continue the same exercise in canter. When you can do this comfortably on both reins then you can raise one of the poles to form a small jump and do the exercise again, in exactly the same way, including the jump. If you are finding this easy then you can raise another pole to form a jump on the other half of the circle.

■ TROTTING TO A FENCE

When you are competing, you should be approaching your fences in canter, but trotting to a fence at home is a very good way to teach your horse to wait and judge the fence and really use himself properly. As he has to tackle the fence with less pace, he will have to make much better use of his technique. It is also very

good for teaching the rider not to anticipate the fence. It is a common fault for the rider to move their upper body forwards before the horse has actually taken off. This unbalances the horse but also makes it very easy for him to stop at the fence as the rider is no longer in a secure position behind the horse.

1 Place a trot pole 2.5–2.7m (8–9 f) from the base of the jump. You can use an x-pole or a small upright. Approach in a positive but balanced trot, allow your horse to find his own way over the trot pole and the jump. Keep your shoulders up and don't anticipate the take off.

2 Let the horse's neck and withers come up to meet you, rather than tipping your body forward to meet the horse. All you need to do is allow the horse to draw your hands forwards as he stretches over the jump. If you can master this then you will always be in a good balance when jumping, rather than getting ahead of the movement and unbalancing your horse.

EVENTING

The sport of eventing, or horse trials or combined training as it is also known, is really a complete test of all-around horsemanship on the part of the rider, and of all-around performance on the part of the horse. Horse and rider are tested on their ability to compete in the disciplines of dressage, show jumping and cross-country. The dressage test demonstrates that the horse is supple, obedient and calm; the show jumping proves his agility and carefulness over fences; the cross-country proves his boldness, speed and stamina. The sport is split into one-day, two-day and three-day events. At a one-day event the order of the phases is usually dressage, show jumping and cross-country. At a three-day event, the cross-country test is held the day after the dressage. The show jumping is held on the final day, testing whether the horse still has the necessary energy, agility, obedience and desire to clear the show jumps following the tough test of his stamina the day before on the speed and endurance phase.

■ HOW THE SPORT DEVELOPED

Eventing was started in Europe by cavalrymen, when they were not away fighting wars. The sport was originally named 'The Military'. It evolved as a way of testing the skills a cavalry horse would need – the dressage represented his suitability for parade duties, the cross-country reflected the need to cross any terrain to seek out, confront or escape the enemy, and the show jumping showed that after the rigours of battle the horse was still fit, willing and obedient, ready to march on to the next challenge.

The first Olympic three-day event was held in 1912. Then and for some years afterwards the sport remained the domain of the military. It spread from country to country through international military competitions and, as events became more numerous, the interest of civilian riders was aroused. Now eventing is a popular sport around the world. Historically, the competition was a far greater test of speed and endurance than it is today, although all three phases in the modern-day sport are technically far more demanding than they used to be.

The early Olympic Eventing competition was only open to male military officers on active service. The different phases were ridden in the

The sport of eventing involves three very different disciplines, all of which must be completed successfully in order to win. The dressage test comes first. While this is simpler than a pure dressage test, it must be remembered that it is being ridden on a horse who has been prepared physically and mentally for the cross-country phase. He knows what is coming next, so it is harder for him to settle for the discipline of dressage.

EQUAL OPPORTUNITIES

Women have been allowed to ride in equestrian events at the Olympics since 1952, and equestrian sports remain one of the very few opportunities that there are for men and women to compete on equal terms against each other. But it wasn't until America's Helena Du Pont rode at the 1964 Tokyo Games that Eventing saw its first female represent her country. Jane Holderness-Roddam (née Bullen) became the first woman to be part of a British Eventing team, winning team gold at the 1968 Mexico Games.

opposite order to today. On the first day, riders completed a 33-mile (53 km) ride and then tackled a 3-mile (4.8 km) cross-country course! The next day they had to complete a steeplechase course, followed by show jumping the next day, and a ten-minute dressage test on the final day.

At the Paris Olympics in 1924, the format was changed to the order that we know today: dressage, then the cross-country test, with show jumping on the last day. Right up until 2004, cross-country day also included additional speed and endurance phases. Riders tackled a set route of roads and tracks, and then rode around a steeplechase course. Another set of roads and tracks took the riders back to a 'ten-minute box' where the horses were checked by a vet (and could be eliminated if they were considered unfit to continue) and also had a chance to be cooled down before setting off over the cross-country test. Each phase had a set time limit, and penalties were incurred for exceeding that limit. This format was known as the 'long

■ OPPOSITE
In one-day events the show-jumping phase comes after the dressage, before the cross-country. At a three-day event it is the final phase, testing the horse's agility and obedience after the rigours and excitement of the cross-country the day before.

format'. In 2004, the 'short format' was introduced, and this is the sport as we know it today. The additional speed and endurance tests were removed, and cross-country day now involves just the cross-country test.

This format has several advantages, the main one being that it involves far less wear and tear on the horses, and this has allowed more horses to continue competing far longer than was previously the case. It is also easier to organize, as it requires far less land, and fewer stewards and helpers. The demise of the long format disappointed many, as it was seen as the ultimate test of horsemanship, and some countries still hold a few long-format competitions, usually at the lower levels, for those wishing to fully test themselves!

■ ONE-DAY AND THREE-DAY EVENTS

At a one-day event you have to complete a dressage test, a course of show jumps and a cross-country course, all on the same day. The penalties incurred in each competition, or phase, are added together, and the winner is the rider incurring the lowest number of penalties. One-day events are an end in themselves for many riders, but their true purpose is to prepare horse and rider for the more demanding two- and three-day events.

A three-day event can actually last for four or five days, depending on the number of entrants. All the horses are stabled together at the event for its duration. Before the competition begins there is a veterinary inspection, where any signs of lameness, injury or illness will result in elimination before you have started. The next one or two days are taken up with everybody completing their dressage tests.

The second part of the competition is the cross-country test. This involves a course of solid obstacles, including natural features such as water crossings, ditches

■ LEFT
The cross-country phase is the most important, and should be the most influential, of the three phases. For most event riders it is the favourite phase.

■ BELOW
Each horse is led up in walk and trot in front of a panel of judges and vets at the start of the three-day event, and also on the morning after the cross-country test, to ensure the horse is fit and well enough to continue in the competition.

and banks. The aim is to try to complete the course without any refusals, falls or runouts, all of which are penalized, within the set optimum time. Exceeding the optimum time incurs time faults which are added to the overall penalty score for each competitor. The higher up the levels you go, the greater the speed, distance and size and number of obstacles.

The morning after the cross-country test, every horse that is still in the competition is inspected and trotted up in front of a panel of vets and judges, who decide whether the horse is fit and well enough to continue to the final phase, which is the show-jumping test. This is usually run in reverse order of merit, so that the overnight leader jumps last. Any penalties incurred for refusals, knock-downs or exceeding the time are added to the dressage and cross-country penalties to give a final score. The winners of three-day events do indeed prove themselves and their horses to be successful, all-around competitors.

■ LEVELS OF COMPETITION

Eventing is governed by the FEI, and there are various levels of affiliated competitions. At international level the sport uses the French name *Concours Complet International* (International Complete Competition) for three-day events, and

Concours International Combiné for one-day events. These titles are abbreviated to CCI and CIC, and are graded from one- to four-star level.

As you progress through the different grades of competition, each phase of dressage, cross-country and show jumping becomes more testing and technical. The cross-country course is between 2600–6840 metres (2843–7480 yards), incorporating 25–45 jumping efforts over solid obstacles. The aim is to complete the course at the speed allocated for each level which, if successfully achieved, means the competitor will finish very close to the optimum time that has been set. At one-

■ RIGHT
As soon as the horse
finishes the cross-
country test, he is
untacked and cooled
down with plenty
of cold water and
walking until he is
fully recovered.

star level the cross-country speed is 520
metres (569 yards) per minute, and at five-
star level it is 570 metres (623 yards) per
minute. Exceeding this optimum time
incurs time faults which are added to the
overall penalty score.

The dimensions of the fences also
become greater, ranging from a height
of 1.5 metres (5 feet) at one-star level, to
1.2 metres (4 feet) on the cross country
and 1.30 metres (4¼ feet) in the show-
jumpiong at fivce-star level. The top
spread can be up to 2 metres (6½ feet).

Each country also holds its own
national one-day events (CNCs), and these
start at a lower level than the CICs. Most
countries offer training and preliminary
competitions with fence dimensions of
between 80 cm and 1 metre (2½ feet to 1
yard), and these serve the purpose of
introducing young horses to the sport
while also offering competition
opportunities to horses and riders who

may not wish to progress to jumping
bigger and more technical obstacles.
There are also Pony Club and Riding Club
events held in most countries.

An interesting aspect of eventing is that
the different competition levels are based
on the ability of the horse, not the rider.
So in a novice (one-star) class you may
find a 16-year-old riding in their first event
on a novice-level horse, competing against
the reigning Olympic champion riding a
novice horse. For many, this is all part of
the charm and attraction of the sport. It is
far more of an achievement to perform
well against experienced riders, even if
you don't win, than it is to take first prize
in a class where you know your rivals
aren't actually that good anyway!

Every horse and rider has to show a
certain level of competence at each level
of the sport before being allowed to move
up to the next level. Equally, in order to
qualify to take part in a CIC or CCI, the

horse and rider must have successfully
completed a number of events as set out
by the FEI rules. This involves achieving
a minimum standard in each phase,
such as scoring over a set percentage in
the dressage, going clear cross-country
with a limited number of time faults, and
achieving no more than 16 jumping
penalties (the equivalent of four fences
down) in the show jumping. This adds
another dimension to the sport, as it
allows you to compete with long-term
goals in mind. You may go to a one-day
event and leave without a prize, but if you
have achieved above the minimum
qualifying score, you are one step closer to
qualifying for your target CIC or CCI.

EQUIPMENT NEEDED

Eventing requires a lot of equipment as
horse and rider need different kit and
equipment for each phase. You can ride all
three phases in one saddle and bridle, but
many horses need a different bit and or
noseband for the different phases. You
should also add a breastplate or girth for
the cross- country phase. If you can afford
a dressage saddle as well as a jumping
saddle it will make a big difference to your
position and effectiveness. You can buy a
saddle with interchangeable flaps for each
discipline as an alternative option. The
horse will need two sets of boots for the
show-jumping and cross-country phases.
For yourself, the same boots, breeches,
shirt, jacket and hat can be worn for the
dressage and show-jumping phases, but for
the cross country you will need a base layer
of some sort and a body protector. At the
higher levels you may wear a tailcoat for
the dressage phase. Check that your hat is
safe and suitable for all three phases. Be
particularly aware that the hat you use for
cross country must not have any form of
peak on it, whereas your dressage or show-
jumping hat can. The best option is to buy
a jockey skull cap with the highest level of
protection and have a blue or black hat
cover for the dressage and show-jumping,
and a coloured cover for the cross country.

■ LEFT
For safe and
successful cross-
country riding, the
horse should be
trained to settle into
a balanced rhythm.
He must be keen to
get to his fences, but
without getting too
excited or too fast.

◼ SKILLS REQUIRED

Bearing in mind what is required for dressage, show jumping and hunter trials will give you some idea of the myriad skills the successful event horse and rider need. But before you are turned off, just think of it in terms of good basic training that equals good all-around performance. If you have put some effort into schooling your horse well on the flat, and have carried through the same principles of rhythm, balance and responsiveness into your jump training, you are well on the way to producing a capable and successful event horse.

Jump training, whether over show jumps or cross-country fences, requires the same technique and skills. The only difference is the speed at which you ride cross-country, and the fact that the natural terrain you have to cross makes it harder to maintain your rhythm and balance than when you are jumping in an arena. An additional factor is the variety of fences you will meet on a cross-country course. Once your horse is familiar with show jumps, he is unlikely to be fazed by anything he meets

◼ **BELOW**
This young horse is showing his inexperience and natural wariness by jumping far bigger than he needs to. It is important that the rider can hold a secure position so that he can stay in balance with the horse if this happens.

in the arena, unless you approach it badly. But the awkward obstacles that can be built into the natural terrain on a cross-country course are numerous, and each time the horse competes he may well be faced with something he has never encountered before.

Cross-country training should concentrate on building up confidence and trust, and making the right decision about the approach you should take.

Fitness is another necessity for both horse and rider. As long as they are regularly hacked out and given some schooling and jump training, most horses and ponies will be fit enough to complete a novice one-day event. Once you want to do more than this, special attention has to be paid to the horse's fitness and training routine. This requires knowledge and experience of how to achieve fitness without subjecting the horse's vulnerable joints and limbs to unnecessary wear and tear. You will also need to be fit, as a tired rider is of little help to a tired horse.

The event rider perhaps needs more determination and persistence than other equestrian competitors, simply because it is a lot harder to get three things to go well all on the same day than it is to get one specialist discipline right.

◼ PRACTISING AT HOME

An event horse has to become really confident about jumping ditches as they are a frequent feature of cross-country courses in many different guises. A big dark hole in the ground is something a horse is quite naturally wary of, so a careful, progressive introduction is needed.

If you have access to a show-jumping water tray you can use this, or you can cut a strip of thick blue or black polythene and use a show-jump pole on each side of it to weigh it down. You can start by leading or lunging your horse over it. Allow him time to look at it and realise it is harmless and then encourage him to step or jump over it. He may give a very big spooky jump so be careful. Then you can ride him over it in trot and finally in canter.

Once he is confident jumping the ditch you can use another show-jump to create a cross country combination such as a coffin or half coffin. Place the show-jump one or two strides away from the ditch and jump them as a combination.

◼ **BELOW**
Despite his first big spooky jump, this horse has soon realised that there is nothing to fear. And after a few more jumps over the ditch, he starts to relax and measure more accurately what he needs to do.

RACE RIDING

Race riding, either on the flat or over fences, offers the best opportunity to experience the full power and speed that a horse can produce. The racing industry revolves around the thoroughbred horse and, to a lesser degree, the Arab horse. Point-to-pointing, the occasional unofficial horse or pony race and the growth in Arab racing all give the amateur rider the chance to experience the thrill of race riding, and the chance to race for the fun of it. Professional jockeys are either retained or employed on a freelance basis by race-horse trainers. They often work for a big training yard in order to supplement their income, exercising and schooling the race horses, as well as racing them competitively if they are offered the ride.

■ POINT-TO-POINTING

This is an amateur sport that tends to thrive wherever hunting thrives. Traditionally, a point-to-point horse had to be qualified by being taken out hunting at least seven times. As it is the local hunts that run the point-to-points, this was a way of them getting extra support from the point-to-point community. But there is much discretion allowed now, as a fit point-to-point horse can find it very difficult to control his enthusiasm when required to stand around in the hunting field. The amateur status of the sport, and the fact that a great many who take part own just one horse that they hunt and

■ LEFT
The ability to sit tight when the unexpected happens is a great asset. Note how this jockey has kept his upper body back and is still looking up and ahead, which is a great aid to keeping in balance when racing.

race, all adds to its fun and social atmosphere. It is popular with spectators, even in winter when they usually end up standing around in the wet and cold, eating a picnic in the car park. There are yards where the owner makes a living out of training and racing either his own or other people's point-to-pointers, and this makes some of the races very competitive.

In most point-to-points the horses jump standard brush fences which may occasionally have a ditch in front, but some courses include banks and water as well. This reflects the sport's origins, when riders simply raced each other from one point, usually a church steeple, to another point somewhere in the distance. Despite its amateur status, the standard of horses and jockeys in point-to-points is ever-increasing. The majority of jockeys and trainers are very professional in their approach to the sport. The member's race is a popular feature at many meetings as this allows the everyday rider, provided he

is a member of the organizing hunt, to take part if so desired.

The point-to-point course is usually an oval-shaped track marked out over an area of grassland. The fences are well spaced out around the course and, because they make use of natural terrain, some courses are much flatter than others. Competitors quickly discover which tracks suit their particular horse best.

■ ARAB RACING

This is a well-organized sport that involves flat races between Arab horses. The racing is fast and competitive, but the sport is still small enough to allow you to train and compete your own horse with success. Races vary in length allowing for pure speed to be tested over the shorter distances and speed and stamina to be tested in the longer races.

EQUIPMENT NEEDED

To race ride you will need lightweight breeches and boots, your racing colours or silks (shirt and hat cover), and a certified jockey helmet and body protector. Goggles are useful – and sometimes essential. A horse can race in an ordinary saddle, but the vast majority will race in a lightweight racing saddle as this makes it easier for the jockey to meet the weight requirement for the race which includes him or her and all his or her tack. A weight cloth is also needed so that the weight to be carried by the horse can be adjusted when necessary.

■ LEFT
Race horses have to be supreme athletes – the greatest care and attention is lavished on them to keep them in peak condition. For a change of scene, these race horses are being exercised on the beach; another day it may be over grass or all-weather gallops, or just hacking along the roads.

■ PONY AND HORSE RACING

There are a few pony and horse races held in most countries that give ordinary riding horses and their jockeys a chance to demonstrate their speed – or lack of it! Most of these are unofficial, although a few countries do have a national body that registers competitors and organizes races for them.

■ PROFESSIONAL FLAT AND JUMP RACING

The international racing scene is divided into flat races, hurdle races, steeplechase races and timber or cross-country races. Flat racing is mainly to test pure speed – many of the races are short sprints where speed rather than stamina count most. Jump racing requires stamina, jumping ability and speed.

◗ BELOW
You can start to increase your lower leg strength and your balance by riding in trot, as well as in canter, with your seat out of the saddle. So even out hacking you can adopt this position when in trot to build your strength and balance. If you feel yourself tipping forwards you will need to raise your upper body a bit more to adjust your balance. If you keep dropping back into the saddle, then you need to bring your upper body forward further forwards. Always lower yourself gently back into the saddle when you finish this exercise rather than bang down hard on your horse's back.

■ SKILLS REQUIRED

In order to race ride you need to be fit, strong and have good balance and a feel for jumping at speed. These can all be practised at home if you intend to race just for fun. But if you want it to be more than that, the best place to learn is in a racing stable, even if you only help out there at weekends. The more thorough-bred race horses you are able to ride, even if only on exercise, the better your fitness, position and balance will become.

■ PRACTISING AT HOME

You will also need to be able to control your weight. Flat-race jockeys, who are often riding two- and three-year-old horses, have to be very lightweight, whereas jump jockeys generally have a higher weight allowance but most still need to keep their weight low enough to ride competitively.

The best way to practise and prepare for race riding is to see if a trainer will let you help ride out his racehorses, even if it's only at weekends. If you are keen to learn and reliable, most racehorse trainers will be delighted to have some extra help. But you can also practise a few skills at home. A strong lower leg position, and good balance are vital in all equestrian sports but are even more important in

SUCCESS IS UP TO YOU

Competing with your horse should be an enjoyable experience for both of you. But riding, and the partnership you have with your horse, has to be worked at. You owe it to your horse to be as good and knowledgeable a rider and owner as you possibly can be. All aspects of his life are in your hands! Never stop trying to improve both yourself and your horse. With the correct help the rider can have a hugely positive influence on the horse. The most ordinary horse can be trained to be extraordinary. My advice to you is; if you are going to ride, strive to ride well. GOOD LUCK!

racing because of the position the jockey rides in. Your seat will be out of the saddle completely when you are galloping and so your lower leg must be strong enough to support not just your body weight, but also the power of the horse pulling against you.

◗ BELOW
If you have some friends you can ride with, and a field to canter in, practise teaching your horse to settle in different positions within the group. Start at the back, and then maybe ride him upsides another horse, then send him to the front. Get a feel for how aware you have to be of the other horses around you, and how you need to time any manoeuvre in order to navigate your way smoothly and safely through a group of horses.

Index

ABOUT THE AUTHOR

Debby Sly has been involved in equestrianism and journalism since graduating from Harper Adams Agricultural College. She worked first as production editor for *What's New in Farming*, before taking over the editorship of *Pony Club Magazine*. For many years Debby was a regular contributor to *Eventing* and *Your Horse* magazines, and has also written many equestrian books, including *Mary Thompson's Eventing Year; Badminton Horse Trials – the triumphs and the tears; Fun with Ponies;* and *The Complete Book of Horses*. With her husband, Martin Ewing, she owned and trained the five star event horse Stormhill Kossack, as well as enjoying Point to Point and Hunter Chase successes. Based in Co Wexford, Ireland, Debby is now mainly involved in training racehorses and point to pointers, as well as specializing in injury rehabilitation.

ACKNOWLEDGEMENTS

The author and photographers would like to thank the following:

Riders: Hector Payne, Yaz Olsson-Sanderson, Aaron Millar, Lou Mesquita, Rachel and Josh Ward, Jessica and Isabel White, Florence Roberts, Amanda Colbourne, Thomas Cooper, Janine Cornish, Charles Daniel, Kate Eckley, Janice Peglar, Sarah Rees-Elford, and Jeremy Russell.

Facilities and equipment: HP Eventing; Aaron Millar Eventing; Alex Van Tuyll; Philip Wellon for the use of land at Vine Farm; Aubiose UK Ltd for the outdoor arena; HAC TAC Ltd for supplying close-contact breeches; and Keenthorne Saddlery, Bridgwater, for clothing and tack.

This edition is published by Lorenz Books, an imprint of Anness Publishing Limited
info@anness.com
www.lorenzbooks.com

© Anness Publishing Ltd 2022

All rights reserved. No part of this publication may be reproduced, stored in a retrieval system, or transmitted in any way or by any means, electronic, mechanical, photocopyint, recording or otherwise, without the prior written permission of the copyright holder.

Publisher: Joanna Lorenz
Editorial Director: Helen Sudell
Additional Photography: Peter Nixon
Designer: Michael Morey
Cover Design: Nigel Partridge
Illustrator: Rodney Paull

PUBLISHER'S NOTE

Although the advice and information in this book are believed to be accurate and true at the time of going to press, neither the author nor the publisher can accept any legal responsibility or liability for any errors or omissions that may have been made nor for any loss, harm or injury that comes about from following instructions or advice in this book.